BRITAIN UNDER THATCHER

Britain under Thatcher

ANTHONY SELDON and
DANIEL COLLINGS

 LONGMAN

An imprint of **PEARSON EDUCATION**

Harlow, England · London · New York · Reading, Massachusetts · San Francisco ·
Toronto · Don Mills, Ontario · Sydney · Tokyo · Singapore · Hong Kong · Seoul ·
Taipei · Cape Town · Madrid · Mexico City · Amsterdam · Munich · Paris · Milan

Wyggeston QEI College
WITHDRAWN
Library

Pearson Education Limited
Edinburgh Gate
Harlow
Essex CM20 2JE
England

and Associated Companies throughout the world

Visit us on the world wide web at:
www.pearsoned-ema.com

First published 2000

© Pearson Education Limited 2000

ISBN 0 582 31714 2 PPR

British Library Cataloguing-in-Publication Data
A catalogue record for this book is available from the British Library

Library of Congress Cataloging-in-Publication Data
Seldon, Anthony.
    Britain under Thatcher / Anthony Seldon and Daniel Collings.
        p. cm. -- (Seminar studies in history)
    Includes bibliographical references and index.
    ISBN 0-582-31714-2
    1. Great Britain--Politics and government--1979–1997.
    2. Thatcher, Margaret. I. Collings, Daniel, 1978– . II. Title
    III. Series.
    DA589.7.S43   1999
    941.085´8--dc21   99-38835
                                                              CIP
    7 6 5 4 3
    05 04 03 02

Set by 7 in 10/12 Sabon
Printed in Malaysia, KVP

CONTENTS

AN INTRODUCTION TO THE SERIES

Such is the pace of historical enquiry in the modern world that there is an ever-widening gap between the specialist article or monograph, incorporating the results of current research, and general surveys, which inevitably become out of date. *Seminar Studies in History* are designed to bridge this gap. The series was founded by Patrick Richardson in 1966 and his aim was to cover major themes in British, European and World history. Between 1980 and 1996 Roger Lockyer continued his work, before handing the editorship over to Clive Emsley and Gordon Martel. Clive Emsley is Professor of History at the Open University, while Gordon Martel is Professor of International History at the University of Northern British Columbia, Canada and Senior Research Fellow at De Montfort University.

All the books are written by experts in their field who are not only familiar with the latest research but have often contributed to it. They are frequently revised, in order to take account of new information and interpretations. They provide a selection of documents to illustrate major themes and provoke discussion, and also a guide to further reading. The aim of *Seminar Studies* is to clarify complex issues without over-simplifying them, and to stimulate readers into deepening their knowledge and understanding of major themes and topics.

NOTE ON REFERENCING SYSTEM

Readers should note that numbers in square brackets [5] refer them to the corresponding entry in the Bibliography at the end of the book (specific page numbers are given in italics). A number in square brackets preceded by *Doc.* [*Doc.* 5] refers readers to the corresponding item in the Documents section which follows the main text.

AUTHORS' ACKNOWLEDGEMENTS

Preparing a manuscript on such a controversial, yet fascinating, subject as Margaret Thatcher has not been an easy task. The authors thus owe a considerable debt to those who have helped with the project in various ways. Many involved in the Thatcher government, at either a ministerial or civil service level, have given invaluable assistance with this book but must remain anonymous: we are nevertheless very grateful for their help.

John Barnes, John Campbell and a third reader have offered shrewd and knowledgeable comments on earlier drafts of the manuscript. We are very grateful to them for generously giving up their valuable time: the finished product has been greatly enhanced by their efforts. Annemarie Weitzel exhibited her usual professionalism in typing selected sections of the text and valuable research work was carried out by Alex Sabine and Peter Snowdon, who both showed considerable judgement and determination. Our thanks also to Sevenoaks Prep and headmaster Edward Oatley for generously allowing us access to their office facilities.

Daniel Collings is fortunate to have benefited from the intellectual insight of Dr Tim Jenkinson and Dr Larry Siedentop, tutors in economics and politics respectively at Keble College, and Dr Jonathan Snicker, tutor in politics at Exeter College, Oxford. He would also like to thank everyone at Keble who has offered their advice, in whatever area, especially Laurence Norman and Ivan Stoyanov, whose incisive analysis helped him to clarify many previously unclear issues. His family also deserve many thanks for their support and help during this project. For help with proof-reading thanks to Paul Thomas, and to Richard Hooper for the index.

The responsibility for any errors that remain lies with the authors alone.

PUBLISHER'S ACKNOWLEDGEMENTS

The publishers would like to thank the following for permission to reproduce copyright material:

The Conservative Party for the poster 'Labour isn't working'; Harper Collins Publishers Ltd for three extracts from *The Downing Street Years* by Margaret Thatcher, and extracts from *Collected Speeches* by Margaret Thatcher; The Thatcher Foundation for extracts from Mrs Thatcher's speech at the 1980 Conservative Party Conference; extracts from *The View from No. 11* by Nigel Lawson, published by Transworld, reprinted by permission of the Peters Fraser & Dunlop Group Limited on behalf of Nigel Lawson; Random House and the Peters Fraser & Dunlop Group Limited for extracts from *Mrs Thatcher's Revolution* by Peter Jenkins; The Controller of Her Majesty's Stationery Office for Ian Gow's memorandum [our Document 7], 'The Single European Act [our Document 15], 'Lawson attacks the Poll Tax' [our Document 24], 'The Bruges Watershed' [our Document 28], Nigel Lawson's resignation letter and Mrs Thatcher's Response [our Document 34], and 'Et tu, Brute?' [our Document 36], together with the Irish Government for the 'Anglo-Irish Agreement: Joint Communiqué [our Document 18], all © Crown copyright; The Controller of Her Majesty's Stationery Office for 'The Falklands Emergency Debate [our Document 9], 'Thatcher Defends Herself' [our Document 21], 'Thatcher Defends the Poll Tax', [our Document 26], 'Healing the Rift' [our Document 27], all © Parliamentary copyright; News International Syndication for extract from *The Sunday Times* article 'Pound to soar as Lawson and Thatcher row' by David Hughes and Christopher Smallwood 13th March 1988 © Times Newspapers Limited 1988, and 'The Keynesian Petition' [our Document 8] from *The Times* dated 30 March 1981 and 'Arthur Scargill Raises the Miners' Spirits' [our Document 17] from *The Times* dated 12 July 1984 ©

Times Newspapers Limited; *The Economist* for 'The Central Policy Review Staff Proposals of 1982' [our Document 12] © *The Economist*, London, 18 September 1982; Independent Newspapers (UK) Ltd for the cartoon 'The Walters Divide' by Nicholas Garland from *The Independent* of 21 July 1988; *The Spectator* for 'Ridley Seals His Fate' [our Document 35] from *The Spectator* dated 14 July 1990; News International Limited for the headline 'You Liar' from *The Sun* [our Document 20].

Whilst every effort has been made to trace the owners of copyright material, in a few cases this has proved problematic and so we take this opportunity to offer our apologies to any copyright holders whose rights we may have unwittingly infringed.

LIST OF ACRONYMS

ABM	Anti-Ballistic Missile
ANC	African National Congress
BBC	British Broadcasting Corporation
BL	British Leyland (later Rover Group)
BR	British Rail
BSC	British Steel Corporation
CAP	Common Agricultural Policy
CBI	Confederation of British Industry
CEGB	Central Electricity Generating Board
CHOGM	Commonwealth Heads of Government Meeting
CND	Campaign for Nuclear Disarmament
CPRS	Central Policy Review Staff
CPS	Centre for Policy Studies
CSCE	Conference on Security and Co-operation in Europe
CTCs	City Technology Colleges
DHA	District Health Authority
DHSS	Department of Health and Social Security
DM	Deutschmark
DoE	Department of the Environment
DTI	Department of Trade and Industry
EC	European Community
ECU	European Currency Unit
EMS	European Monetary System
EMU	European Monetary Union
ERM	Exchange Rate Mechanism (of the EMS)
FCO	Foreign and Commonwealth Office
G7	Group of Seven
GATT	General Agreement on Tariffs and Trade
GCHQ	Government Communications Headquarters
GDP	Gross Domestic Product

GLC	Greater London Council
GM	General Motors
GM schools	grant-maintained schools
GNP	Gross National Product
GP	General Practitioner
HAT	Housing Action Trust
IEA	Institute of Economic Affairs
IGC	Inter-governmental Conference
IMF	International Monetary Fund
INF	Intermediate-range Nuclear Forces
INLA	Irish National Liberation Army
IRA	Irish Republican Army
LEA	Local Education Authority
M0	Monetary Base
MAD	Mutually Assured Destruction
MoD	Ministry of Defence
MP	Member of Parliament
MTFS	Medium-term financial strategy
NACODS	National Association of Colliery Overmen, Deputies and Shotfirers
NADs	National Armaments Directors
NATO	North Atlantic Treaty Organisation
NCB	National Coal Board (later British Coal)
NHS	National Health Service
NUM	National Union of Mineworkers
OECD	Organisation for Economic Co-operation and Development
OECS	Organisation of Eastern Caribbean States
OPEC	Organisation of Petroleum Exporting Countries
PA	Press Association
PM	Prime Minister
PPS	Parliamentary Private Secretary
PSBR	Public Sector Borrowing Requirement
QC	Queen's Counsel
Quango	Quasi-autonomous non-governmental organisation
RPI	Retail Price Index
RUC	Royal Ulster Constabulary
SAS	Special Air Service
SDI	Strategic Defence Initiative
SDP	Social Democratic Party
SEA	Single European Act
SERPS	State earnings-related pension scheme

SNF	Short-range Nuclear Forces
TGWU	Transport and General Workers Union
TUC	Trades Union Congress
UK	United Kingdom
UNSCR	United Nations Security Council Resolution
US(A)	United States (of America)
VAT	Value Added Tax

To Edward H. Oatley and Russell D. Tillson,
inspiring teachers

PART ONE: INTRODUCTION

1   THE ROAD TO 1979

When Margaret Hilda Roberts was born on 13 October 1925, Stanley Baldwin was the Conservative Prime Minister. Her parents had both been born when Conservative premiers were in power. She went to Oxford when the great Conservative war leader, Winston Churchill, was Prime Minister, and the year she married Denis Thatcher, 1951, saw Churchill return to defeat Labour and usher in thirteen years of Tory rule. She became an MP in 1959, representing Finchley, when another long-serving Conservative, Harold Macmillan, was premier, and under him, and later the aristocratic Tory Prime Minister, Alec Douglas-Home (1963–64), became a junior government minister. She was truly a product of the Conservative century, while her own subsequent political career helped ensure that the Tory domination of the century would continue over its last two decades.

MRS THATCHER'S POLITICAL RISE

Mrs Thatcher's promotion through the party was swift. Her diligence, single-mindedness, intelligence and immense capacity for hard work, as well as her indisputable loyalty, made her an inevitable candidate for senior office, overcoming whatever obstacles might have been posed by her gender and her lack of public school education and membership of 'old boy' networks. Appointed to 'shadow' the education area when the Labour Prime Minister Harold Wilson was in power, she became Education Secretary after the June 1970 general election.

The new Conservative Prime Minister, Edward Heath, left her a largely free hand [20 *p. 447*] and she became a capable if occasionally controversial Education Secretary, most notably by abolishing free school milk to all primary children aged over seven, which resulted in her first serious attack from media and public as 'Thatcher, the milk snatcher'. What tends to be forgotten is that she agreed this cut only to save the Open University. Some elements of her later ideological stances could be detected at this time, notably a suspicion of civil servants for being 'socialist' [29 *p. 166*] and the doubts she raised about parts of the 1972 Industrial Expansion Act, which made too many concessions to socialism for her liking. But she also battled with Cabinet to increase the education budget, and gave little indication, other than her acute tenacity and an impatience with waste and incompetence, of her future quality and outlook.

CHALLENGE FOR THE PARTY LEADERSHIP (FEBRUARY 1975)

The loss of the February 1974 election, and Heath's failure to adopt new ideas in opposition, proved decisive turning points for Mrs Thatcher. Granted more time to think by being relieved of office, Mrs Thatcher threw herself into a ferment of intellectual analysis. What, she asked herself, had gone wrong with government: why was it so incapable, as proved by the administrations of both Wilson and Heath, of running an efficient economy, keeping down inflation, and standing up to trade unions? Key in this process of analysis was the new office or 'think tank', the Centre for Policy Studies (CPS) that was founded in 1974. Mrs Thatcher and Keith Joseph played an important role in the early activities of the CPS, and to Heath's annoyance, Mrs Thatcher became its vice chairman that June. Joseph had been another high-spending minister under Heath during 1970–74 (as Health and Social Security Secretary) but travelled his own 'road to Damascus' very shortly after the February 1974 election defeat. He later spoke about scales being removed from his eyes to allow him at last to see the truth, which was all about 'escaping the chrysalis of socialism' [70 *p. 16*].

Joseph was very important to Mrs Thatcher's own political development, as she later was fulsomely to acknowledge, although the first roots for what was to become Thatcherism probably date back to her earlier associations with the Institute of Economic Affairs (IEA), a right-wing think tank. Joseph helped her to see the limitations of the Keynesian social democratic, consensus-style thinking which had characterised government policy since 1945 [62 *p. 152*], and which had been pursued by both Labour and Conservative governments. The size of the state sector as a result had risen inexorably year on year, giving great power to civil servants, but choking, he argued, the private sector and individual freedom. In the place of 'consensus' policies, Joseph was attracted to an alternative set of policy prescriptions, dating back to the classical economists of the nineteenth century and earlier, but championed more recently by thinkers like F. A. Hayek and economists like Milton Friedman, by international bodies like The Mont Pelerin Society (founded 1947) and in Britain by the Institute of Economic Affairs (IEA, founded 1957).

The new thinking – not all of which saw the light of day at this time – saw big government as the problem, not (as socialists believe) the solution. At its heart was a commitment to monetarism: the view that the sole cause of inflation was the willingness of government to create an excessive money supply. It rejected the notion that wage increases were the ultimate cause of inflation and hence that incomes policies – unpopular and often politically disastrous for their creators – were necessary or effective to control it.

Excessive trade union power was seen as an important cause of Britain's industrial decline relative to its rivals. Dropping incomes policy would make it possible to reform the trade unions since union acquiescence in economic policy would cease to be necessary, and so the balance of power in industry could be switched back from unions to management – a prospect that generated support for monetarism among Conservatives and others who had no interest in, or understanding of, economic theory.

The final component of the new thinking was a general attack on public expenditure and the huge state sector, which made up over 20% of the British economy in 1979. By controlling public spending while the economy grew, taxes could be cut and profits and incentives to enterprise restored. Inefficient state monopolies in the nationalised industries would be sold into the private sector and opened up to private sector disciplines, reducing state subsidies and possibly even generating tax revenue. The welfare state would be subject to reform to increase incentives to work and remove (or reduce) dependency, helping to contain public spending. What Keith Joseph called the 'ratchet effect' of socialism would be checked and then reversed.

All this was radical stuff, and complete anathema to Heath and other traditional Tories. It appealed to neither the traditional moderate, 'One Nation' Tories, nor indeed to the traditional 'old' right wing, which had strong upper-class roots and which hankered after a vision of Britain as head of a great empire run by all-knowing Tories. But it was the loss of the second election, in October 1974, and Heath's continuing aloofness from his backbenchers, rather than an ideological reaction against his consensual brand of 'One Nation' Conservatism that finally sealed Heath's fate. After that second election defeat a leadership election became almost inevitable.

When Joseph decided that he himself was unsuitable to challenge Heath for the leadership, and when Edward Du Cann, Chairman of the '1922 Committee' of Conservative backbenchers, ruled himself out for personal reasons, Joseph's protégé, Mrs Thatcher, took up the cudgels and announced that she would take on Heath. Mrs Thatcher's position in the leadership stakes, and her self-esteem, were bolstered by her commanding performance in the House during the debates on the Finance Bill during the winter of 1974–75. Her campaign platform, however, proved to be cautious in terms of specific policies, although she was not afraid of making her distinctive Tory first principles clear. However, little emphasis was placed on these principles, as many Tory MPs and commentators doubted she would act on her rhetoric. Her platform was thus perceived as cautious with a stress on the new consultative style of leadership that she promised.

The first round of the leadership election in February 1975 saw her achieve the votes of 130 Tory MPs as against Heath's 119, a clear indication that the Parliamentary party wanted a change of leader, but not necessarily that they wanted Mrs Thatcher. The ultra-safe Old Wykehamist, chairman of the party, and key establishment figure of William Whitelaw was her most senior challenger in the second round. She won with 146 votes, less because of approval (or even much understanding) of her new political creed and more due to a rejection of the past (Whitelaw was a 'One Nation' Tory, and very closely identified with Heath) and the highly skilful management of her campaign by the Tory MP Airey Neave. As the commentator Peter Riddell wrote: 'Mrs Thatcher became leader of the Conservative Party in February 1975 principally because she was not Edward Heath, not because of a widespread commitment to her views. She was the only senior candidate willing to challenge Mr Heath at a time when the majority of Tory MPs wanted a change' [66 *p. 21*].

PREPARING FOR POWER (1975–79)

Mrs Thatcher had become the first ever woman to lead the Tory Party, and to the surprise of many had won by a comfortable margin. But she had far from won over the party to her thinking. The struggle for the intellectual hegemony of the party was to be aptly dubbed in the early years of her government as a struggle between the 'dries', the allegedly hard-nosed figures like Mrs Thatcher and Keith Joseph who thought that uncompromising measures were necessary before Britain recovered its economic position, not to mention moral fibre, and the 'wets' or 'One Nation' Tories, who preferred the Keynesian-style policies of Macmillan, Home and Heath, and who were not prepared to institute tough measures if it meant unemployment or social disadvantage rising to unacceptably high levels.

The balance in Mrs Thatcher's 'Shadow Cabinet' was undoubtedly 'wet'. Only two key Heath figures left the Shadow Cabinet, Robert Carr and Peter Walker, and the body remained unashamedly full of 'Heathites'. Very few were subscribers to the new thinking, Keith Joseph, Geoffrey Howe, Angus Maude and John Biffen being prominent among this minority. The heavyweights – Whitelaw, Ian Gilmour, Lord Carrington, Francis Pym, Jim Prior – were almost all wets. She came under attack, from outside her Shadow Cabinet, from Peter Walker, for putting too much belief in monetarist economics in 1976, and from insiders such as Gilmour, who disliked her attempt to implant, as they saw it, unwelcome strands of 'alien' thinking into traditional Tory Party philosophy. Heath attacked her too, with increasing bitterness, but over time he lost credibility and came to be seen as a bad loser.

Mrs Thatcher thus had to move stealthily, coaxing and cajoling her Shadow Cabinet behind her. The 1976 policy statement *The Right Approach* was followed in 1977 by *The Right Approach to the Economy*, committing the party to a more free enterprise line than many 'wets' would have liked, but refusing to rule out an incomes policy and falling short of the thoroughgoing capitalism and anti-trade unionism the more ardent 'dries' and free enterprise think tanks like the CPS and IEA were advocating.

While the Tories hounded the Labour government of James Callaghan, who succeeded Wilson as Prime Minister in April 1976, their task became easier both due to Callaghan's loss of a parliamentary majority, and to internal Labour divisions over economic policy and devolution. Policy groups and discussions had been taking place in earnest during 1976 and 1977, although Mrs Thatcher was anxious to avoid what she considered to be Heath's mistake during his own period as opposition leader (1965–70) of producing too many *detailed* policies. By mid-1978, a draft manifesto was written in the likely event of an autumn election, which polls showed, after dreadful showings in 1976 and 1977, that Labour had a chance of winning. But, to general surprise, Callaghan decided to delay the election until the following year, eventually being forced to call it when he lost a Commons vote of confidence at the end of March 1979.

THE 1979 ELECTION

The Conservatives' 1979 manifesto, uninspiringly entitled *The Conservative Manifesto 1979*, was, as Mrs Thatcher wished, high on general principle, but light on specific commitments. There was, for example, no specific pledge to 'privatise' (i.e. return to private ownership) any of the large number of nationalised industries. The manifesto did, however, promise to reduce government spending, to toughen rules governing trade unions, and to control the money supply (monetarism). The delay in calling the general election until after the winter proved to be a fatal procrastination for Labour. The trade unions rebelled against the Labour government's attempt to hold down wages with their incomes policy, and high-profile strikes during the 'winter of discontent', for example by lorry drivers, hospital porters and grave diggers, gave the impression of a government, and a country, out of control.

The delay in the date of the election until 3 May gave the Conservatives a chance to revise their draft manifesto, notably by a toughening of passages on trade unions in reaction to the 'winter of discontent'. The loss of government authority, a theme of the whole 1970s, but underlined by the events of the previous winter, had played largely into Mrs Thatcher's hands. She could portray the Tories as the party of law and order, offering Britain a new start after a prolonged period of chaos amounting almost to anarchy. 'Popular capitalism' was dangled before the electorate with promises of sharp cuts in income tax and the prospect of tenants being able to buy their own council houses, the latter a proposal put to, and rejected by, Callaghan. Furthermore, building on the highly effective 'Labour isn't working' poster, devised by the advertising agency Saatchi and Saatchi and which first appeared in the summer of 1978, the Tories continued to strike at one of Labour's most sacred promises, to be the party to protect the working class [*Doc. 1*].

In the election, the Conservatives won 339 seats to Labour's 269, with the Tories' percentage of the vote compared to October 1974 rising from 35.8 per cent to 43.9 per cent, the largest swing of votes away from the other main party between 1945 and 1997. Mrs Thatcher won with an overall majority of 43. Yet, as studies showed [38 *p. 340*], the election result was better explained by a discredited government losing the election rather than a challenger winning it on the back of a popular fresh set of policies. As Mrs Thatcher had found after she became party leader in February 1975, winning was only the beginning of her struggles: she still had much left to prove, and many 'enemies' to outwit.

PART TWO: ANALYSIS

2 ESTABLISHING HEGEMONY

APPOINTING A GOVERNMENT (1979)

At 2.45 pm on 4 May 1979 Margaret Thatcher was called to Buckingham Palace to be asked by the Queen to form a government. By 11 pm that evening the new Prime Minister had finalised the composition of her first Cabinet: within 48 hours the ministers of state and junior ministers had been decided and with it the final composition of the team that would launch her premiership.

Four years of hard work as opposition leader, against first Harold Wilson and from April 1976 James Callaghan, had paved the way for this hour. The period had been formative, honing both her free market view on policy and also her unequivocal views of leadership. By 1979 she seemed to be ready to force her own ideas on the party, stating in a celebrated interview for *The Observer* that 'it must be a conviction government. As PM I could not waste time having any internal arguments' [6 25.2.79].

However, her bold claim fell short of the reality of much of her first administration (1979-83). Although, despite press speculation [1 5.5.79], Heath himself was not appointed, a broad spectrum of party opinion was represented in the 1979 Cabinet. Her Cabinet was largely a replica of the Shadow Cabinet that she led into the 1979 election, with a large proportion of the personnel transferred, even if they did not all hold the same posts.

The Cabinet thus contained a strong representation of Heathites, such as Lord Carrington (Foreign Secretary), Jim Prior (Employment), Francis Pym (Defence), Ian Gilmour (Lord Privy Seal), Michael Heseltine (Environment), Norman St. John Stevas (Arts) and Mark Carlisle (Education). Of particular significance was the appointment of Peter Walker as Minister of Agriculture as Walker was a very close friend of Heath and had not been included in her Shadow Cabinet. Mrs Thatcher explains Walker's appointment in her memoirs: 'His membership of the Cabinet demonstrated that I was prepared to include every strand of Conservative opinion in the new Government, [on the other hand,] his post [demonstrated] that I was not prepared to put the central economic strategy at risk' [28 *p. 28*].

Her point about the 'central economic strategy' is indicative. While only a minority of the Cabinet shared Mrs Thatcher's own free market ideas, this minority was strategically placed to ensure that she and her acolytes retained control of what she considered most important: economic policy.

Geoffrey Howe was thus appointed Chancellor of the Exchequer. Howe had been Shadow Chancellor since the leadership election in 1975, was a Thatcher loyalist, and had established firm monetarist credentials by his willingness to call for both public expenditure and tax cuts to counter Britain's economic difficulties. Support for Mrs Thatcher's objectives at the Treasury was bolstered by the appointment of John Biffen as Chief Secretary to the Treasury, another believer in monetarism who had added appeal in Mrs Thatcher's eyes in that he had been a 'courageous critic of the Heath Government's U-turn' [28 *p. 26*].

The man who had the greatest intellectual input in shaping her thinking, at least in economic policy, Keith Joseph, was discounted for the post of Chancellor, apparently on the grounds that his own character made it difficult for him to be sufficiently effective and ruthless [28 *p. 26*]. Instead, he was appointed to the second key economic job, Industry Secretary. It was envisaged that from here he would support the Treasury in cutting back industrial interventions, anathema to the Thatcherite economic policy that Joseph had played a key part in establishing.

Mrs Thatcher further bolstered her hegemony over economic policy by the appointment of two more confirmed monetarists to the key posts of Trade Secretary and Energy Secretary, which were given to John Nott and David Howell respectively. In addition to these supporters in Cabinet, two further appointments were to prove vital to her. The first, ironically, was a man who did not subscribe to the monetarist canon: William Whitelaw. Since he had been beaten by Mrs Thatcher in the 1975 leadership contest, Whitelaw had been Deputy leader handling devolution until November 1976 before becoming Home Affairs spokesman. Appointed Home Secretary in 1979, he became *de facto* Deputy Prime Minister. Whitelaw had served in every Conservative government since Harold Macmillan (1957-63) and had developed a reputation for being a very perceptive judge of what the Parliamentary party would stomach and for knowing what Tory MPs really thought. He now coupled these clubbable skills with his wide-ranging experience and an unshakable loyalty to the new Prime Minister, thus proving an invaluable source of support and advice in the years to come. It is perhaps no coincidence that when, after nine-and-a-half years, he withdrew from government, the Prime Minister began to lose her way.

The second appointment was that of Ian Gow as Mrs Thatcher's Parliamentary Private Secretary, a non-ministerial job whose purpose is to be the 'eyes and ears' of the Prime Minister with Tory MPs, and to help explain the one to the other. Like Whitelaw, Gow knew the party very well, and was a regular in the House of Commons' tea room. Gow not only succeeded in keeping Mrs Thatcher in regular touch with party opinion, but was also very effective in persuading potential dissenters of the wisdom of the leader's course of action.

It should also be noted that initially Mrs Thatcher was suspicious of the civil service and intent on using her Policy Unit, headed by John Hoskyns, and other political advisors as much as possible. However, she soon came to rely on her own officials at Number Ten, though she continued to harbour reservations about some senior officials in the Treasury and even more so in the Foreign Office. In short, when taken as a whole, Mrs Thatcher's appointments did not establish the kind of hegemony she had hinted at prior to the election. However, she did ensure that effective opposition to her economic plans would be ineffective, and this was confirmed by the course of Mrs Thatcher's first year in office.

ECONOMIC BATTLES: THE FIRST BUDGET AND ECONOMIC STRATEGY (1979–80)

Mrs Thatcher was determined to use the first Queen's Speech, on 15 May 1979, to spell out clearly that her government meant business. Examples include social policy, where council house tenants would be given the right to buy their homes, and education policy, where there would be no compulsion for local authorities to replace grammar schools with comprehensives and the 'Assisted Places Scheme' would be introduced, providing grants on a selective basis for children from poor backgrounds to attend independent schools. The four areas that were discussed in the speech that were to be most vigorously pursued in the first year were: economic policy, industrial relations, relations with the European Community (EC) and Rhodesia.

Economic policy provided the first real evidence of the willingness of the Thatcher government to put its radical policies into effect. In Howe's first Budget, on 12 June, the Chancellor looked to implement the government's declared policies of reducing inflation through control of the money supply and cutting income tax to stimulate the private sector. The top rate of income tax was cut from 83 to 60 pence in the pound and the lower rate was reduced from 33 to 30 pence. This income tax cut was to be accompanied by a reduction of £4 billion in public expenditure, but to enable the direct tax cuts to be accommodated, VAT, an indirect tax on goods and services, had to rise from the two rates of 8% and 12.5% to one unified rate of 15%. The Budget also set interest rates at 14% and took the first steps in abolishing exchange controls that limited the amount of foreign currency British citizens could acquire and tightly limited overseas travel. The abolition of exchange controls was a very bold reform and probably the government's most important move in exposing the British economy to a global market.

The Budget was more radical than had been expected by many financial experts [1 *13.6.79*]. Particularly unexpected were the extent of the public expenditure cuts and the high level of VAT (a 12.5% unified rate had been the common prediction). It is certainly true that the decision to pursue such a radical course was not taken lightly, and when Howe first proposed the 15% rate Mrs Thatcher was concerned about the increase in the Retail Price Index (and thus in inflation) that would result. At a meeting on 24 May, however, Howe and his leader finally agreed the essential details of the Budget with the decisive argument being that such a radical switch from direct to indirect taxation could only be enacted while the general election mandate remained fresh. Howe notes that there was no 'significant prior discussion of the Budget in Cabinet' [21 *p. 133*]. Although it is true that the details of Budgets themselves are never discussed in Cabinet for fear of leaks, Howe is referring to the fact that the government's general economic strategy was being determined by a small inner core of loyal ministers, whose views were in a minority in Cabinet. When Heathite ministers such as Prior, Walker and Gilmour finally learned the Budget's details, on the day that Howe delivered it, they were horrified. Prior was especially distressed as he had warned Mrs Thatcher that a high rate of VAT would be inflationary, as wage claims would rise to reflect the higher cost of living (not an analysis a monetarist would share, of course). Inflation was further boosted by the huge rise of £1.25 billion in public sector wage settlements [64 *p. 444*] which resulted from the recommendations of the Clegg Commission on pay in the public sector – a legacy of the past government which the Tories had committed themselves to honour during the election campaign. Despite rising inflation, which was to double in Mrs Thatcher's first year, the government's claim that it would be reduced through control of the money supply was sustained and thus interest rates were raised to an unprecedented 17% on 18 November. The economic policy of the first year culminated in the announcement of the medium-term financial strategy (MTFS) in the 1980 Budget, again without a full Cabinet economic discussion beforehand. The monetarist MTFS laid out the aim of bringing down inflation by decreasing monetary growth while preventing excessively high interest rates by decreasing government borrowing. Therefore, whatever the economic consequences, during her first year Mrs Thatcher demonstrated her personal hegemony and that of her ideas in economic policy.

A BUSY FIRST YEAR (1979-80)

Early Union Clashes

The second plank of the 1979 Queen's Speech concerned the unions. Mrs Thatcher had decided that her government would not operate an incomes policy and instead looked to control wage settlements by bringing the unions within the scope of the law. Although Mrs Thatcher was initially cautious in her approach to trade union reform, remembering the failures of Heath's Industrial Relations Act, this attitude did not last. She asked the Employment Secretary, Jim Prior, to present his view on the best way to proceed with trade union reform. Prior's plans required 80% of employees in the workplace to agree before a 'closed shop' could be declared, provided funds for postal ballots of union members and outlawed secondary picketing. Prior's method of advance on this notoriously difficult ground of the 1970s was to hold delicate union consultations to obtain the backing of the more moderate union leaders while stressing that his legislation would fulfil the manifesto commitments. Although Mrs Thatcher was content to go along with this approach at first, when the Iron and Steel Trades Confederation called its members out on strike on 2 January 1980 over a pay dispute, backbench impatience with union reform became evident. This pressure found much sympathy with the Prime Minister and she called for Prior's legislation to be strengthened and secondary picketing to be made illegal immediately.

Prior successfully resisted her demands, however, and the 1980 Employment Act bore a very close resemblance to Prior's original proposals. Those calling for a more radical attack on union privileges had to wait for the 1982 Employment Act, passed under Prior's more aggressive successor, Norman Tebbit, which made unions liable for damages in the case of unlawful industrial action. However, even at this early stage, Mrs Thatcher appeared to establish a firm government policy for dealing with strikes. This took the form of a 'demonstration effect' [76 p. 195], where the dispute was allowed to run on to the bitter end, without the government bowing to union demands or providing extra money. Despite the 13-week struggle and the 6% unconditional pay rise that the unions finally obtained after an independent enquiry into wages was established (the management had proposed 2%), Mrs Thatcher believed that the government had made an effective start in a policy that would eventually lead to the establishment of hegemony over the trade unions.

EC budget wrangles

But it was not only in domestic policy that Mrs Thatcher chose to use the first year to stamp her authority. She decided that Britain's financial contribution to the European Community needed urgent attention. It was estimated by the Treasury that Britain would make a £1,000 million net contribution to the EC in 1979, making Britain the largest contributor despite her income being less than the EC average. For Mrs Thatcher there were huge advantages to fighting on this ground: Europeans were taking excessive British money and thus depriving British tax payers of improvements to their own public services. This fight against Europe was thus perfect territory in which to stir up populism at home. Although she later wrote that the attitude towards the future of Europe of some European leaders was 'interventionist, protectionist, and ultimately federalist' [28 p. 61], at the time there was little talk of European federalism. Her battle was fought only on the need to reduce the budget contribution: her wider concerns about the EC came much later in her premiership.

Having staked out her ground, a significant reduction in the British contribution, both informally to various European leaders and more formally at the June Strasbourg Summit and in her Churchill Memorial Lecture in Luxembourg in October, the first real test of her nerve came at the Dublin Summit in November. Here both European leaders and experienced officials from the Foreign Office were surprised, shocked even, by her aggressive and stubborn form of diplomacy. In the past, EC Summits had been at least calm and reasoned on the surface, if fairly Machiavellian beneath. Furthermore, when Mrs Thatcher was offered a £350 million refund, she rejected it as too small and the Summit appeared in danger of breaking up without even agreeing to a further meeting. However further talks were agreed to at the end of the meeting and these took place at the Luxembourg Summit on 27 April 1980. It appeared that Mrs Thatcher's uncompromising style had paid off as she was offered a refund of £760 million, but again she rejected the deal (to the fury of her European partners) essentially on the grounds that it would only last for two years and she wanted a more permanent solution. A deal was finally brokered by Foreign Secretary Carrington and Gilmour (Lord Privy Seal) at an EC Foreign Ministers' meeting in Brussels in May. The deal thus brought back for Mrs Thatcher's approval involved an increase in the refund of some £60 million, but crucially it was to be a three-year solution rather than just lasting for two.

Despite Carrington and Gilmour's enthusiasm for the deal, Mrs Thatcher was still reluctant to accept it as she felt the figures had been fudged and Britain's refund would actually be less than had been available at Luxembourg. She nevertheless did finally accept it, claiming to be pleased with a three-year solution. Speculation has arisen as to quite why she did agree to settle at this point, especially as she was gaining capital from continuing to ride the wave of anti-EC populism which also distracted attention from domestic problems. It seems likely, however, that she was forced to accept the deal as not only did Carrington and Gilmour threaten to resign if the settlement was rejected, but the Cabinet swung behind the deal, leaving Mrs Thatcher isolated [*Docs. 2 and 3*].

Rhodesian independence

The first year also saw a solution to the long-running Rhodesian problem. Rhodesia was a British colony that had been an irritant to successive governments since the Prime Minister, Ian Smith, who headed a white minority government, had declared unilateral independence in 1965. World opinion refused to accept Smith's regime as legitimate as blacks were to be denied the vote, and economic sanctions had been imposed on the country while, inside Rhodesia, black rebels fought a civil war against Smith's government. In 1979, elections were held under a new, more democratic constitution and the black bishop, Abel Muzorewa, was elected as Prime Minister. It was argued, however, that the new regime was not legitimate as the constitution under which the elections had taken place served only to entrench white power and the black nationalists of the Patriotic Front (led by Joshua Nkomo and Robert Mugabe) had not taken part. Muzorewa was thus seen as little more than a front for Smith.

However, Mrs Thatcher faced a dilemma over this notoriously prickly issue for Tory leaders, where the right of the party still did not accept the principle of 'one man: one vote' in Africa. Several right-wing Conservative MPs were supporters of Smith, and as Smith had made some concessions their calls for Rhodesia to be at last recognised became more persuasive, particularly as independent monitors reported that the 1979 elections had been fairly conducted. There were also risks in supporting the Patriotic Front, whom many, including Mrs Thatcher, regarded as terrorists. She thus had a number of reasons for recognising the new regime. However, Mrs Thatcher was persuaded that as long as the rest of the world failed to recognise the regime, there was little chance of the civil war being brought to an end – a necessary prelude to the lifting of sanctions.

At the 1979 Lusaka Commonwealth Conference she began what historian Kenneth Morgan terms a 'huge surrender' [64 *p. 451*], bowing to the pressure from the Foreign Office and Commonwealth leaders, and agreeing that the current Rhodesian Constitution should be scrapped and a new version drafted. She also agreed to recognise the legitimacy of the Patriotic Front and ensured that Britain would take full responsibility for organising the new constitution and putting its provisions into place. If she had been unsure of the best course of action before Lusaka, after it she was determined that what had been agreed would be carried through effectively. This led to a Constitutional Conference at Lancaster House in September 1979, attended by all Rhodesia's rival leaders. Although this was chaired by Carrington, Mrs Thatcher played an important role in keeping other countries up to date with the progress that was made and exerting pressure behind the scenes. The outcome bore all the marks of a diplomatic triumph. Lord Soames, Churchill's son-in-law and a former British Ambassador in Paris, now a junior member of her Cabinet, was sent out to act as Governor for a transitional period. Free elections were duly held, and Robert Mugabe was elected Prime Minister. Although the Rhodesian solution was a diplomatic success, it was ironic that such an ardent anti-Communist had helped a Marxist to gain power.

TOUGH GOING: VANQUISHING THE 'WETS' (1980–81)

Although Margaret Thatcher had shown herself able and willing to implement the economic policies she believed in during the first year, during 1980 Britain's economic situation seemed only to worsen. In 1980 there was a fall in manufacturing production of 16%, the Retail Price Index (RPI) rose by 20% between May 1979 and May 1980 and unemployment, 1,288,000 and falling when the Conservatives took office, reached 2 million by November. As a deep recession appeared to take hold in spite of (some commentators like William Keegan said because of) Mrs Thatcher's policies, her opponents felt more confident in airing their doubts about her whole strategy [60; for an alternative view, see: 75].

After relative harmony in her first year, Cabinet meetings now became more divided and the strong reservations of the 'wets' regarding the government's whole economic strategy [*Doc. 4*], which were aired during Cabinet economic discussions and the public spending rounds in July 1980, soon found their way into the press. These divisions and leaks continued and during the October Party Conference several 'wets' made speeches which, while falling short of criticism, contained subtle asides that were intended to influence the government, such as St. John Stevas talking about the dangers of 'theoreticians living in an abstract world' [*76 p. 208*]. Mrs Thatcher struck back with the now famous phrase, provided by her speech writer and playwright, Ronnie Millar, and which came to sum up her whole tough leadership style, in contrast to Heath's vacillations: 'U-turn if you want to, the lady's not for turning' [*30 p. 116*] [*Doc. 5; Doc. 6*].

After further Cabinet clashes on public expenditure in October and November, during which Pym threatened resignation, Mrs Thatcher decided she needed to reassert her authority over the Cabinet dissenters. The reshuffle of 5 January 1981 saw St. John Stevas, an outspoken 'wet', and belittling of her in private, leave the government, Mrs Thatcher believing that he had 'turned indiscretion into a political principle' [*28 p. 130*]. The 'wets' also lost control of the Ministry of Defence, as John Nott replaced Francis Pym, who moved sideways to become Leader of the House. John Biffen took over from Nott at Trade and Leon Brittan, a close friend of Howe, entered the Cabinet as Chief Secretary to the Treasury. At the same time, in a key move little commented upon at the time, the arch monetarist Alan Walters was appointed to her personal staff at Number Ten as her personal economic advisor. However, any increase in morale generated by this first reshuffle of 1981 was short lived as the government faced continuing woes.

Very soon after the reshuffle, the government faced a challenge from the coal industry. Early in 1981, the National Coal Board (NCB) informed the government of its plans for the closure of uneconomic pits. These plans were certain to provoke strikes from the National Union of Mineworkers (NUM), the union having been in the vanguard of the massive union unrest that had been the leitmotif of the 1970s. At first the Department of Energy agreed with the Board that there was no alternative but to close the pits, and David Howell, Energy Secretary, reported this to Mrs Thatcher at the end of January.

However, by the next month Howell had changed his view and explained to the Prime Minister that he now believed that the government's aim should be to avoid a strike at all costs. Because stocks of coal at power stations were simply not great enough to endure a long strike, Mrs Thatcher was forced to agree that there was no alternative at this stage but to give in to the NUM's demands. After a tripartite meeting with the NUM and the NCB, Howell therefore announced to the Commons that the government pledged to ensure that imports of coal were as low as possible and to review the financial constraints on the coal industry. In return the NCB agreed to postpone the closure plans.

The government's hard rhetoric of resistance when faced with industrial action had thus been tested and found wanting. The result was a further erosion of morale inside the Parliamentary party, already vexed by recession and rising unemployment. This is illustrated by a memorandum that Gow sent to Mrs Thatcher on 27 February in which he reported that the perceived defeat over coal, combined with severe doubts over economic policy, had led to a 'noticeable deterioration in the morale of our backbenchers' [28 *p. 132*] [*Doc. 7*]. This memorandum reached Mrs Thatcher less than two weeks before Howe's seminal 1981 Budget was due to be delivered. But she had already decided that this Budget could not be an exercise in morale boosting: indeed, it was to have the opposite effect.

As Britain entered the deep recession, instead of following the course urged by orthodox Keynesians – allowing public spending to rise and borrowing more to finance it – the government chose to *cut* borrowing by raising taxes. Keynesians argued that such policies would deepen the recession, but supporters argued that lower public borrowing would enable interest rates to be reduced from their very high level, reducing the level of sterling (also very high) and so help industry recover from the recession. Behind the scenes, there were arguments between monetarists as to how best to measure the money supply, some believing that the existing policy had been based on the wrong measure and that it had involved a large measure of overkill. On this point of view, reducing interest rates had to be the government's highest priority.

Mrs Thatcher certainly wanted interest rates brought down, but initially she had doubts as to the wisdom of raising taxes in the face of recession, though more for political than economic reasons. However, in the end she came down firmly in favour of tax increases, while realising how unpopular the Budget would be. The Budget left the rate of income tax unchanged, but tax thresholds were not raised in line with inflation and duties on tobacco, alcohol and petrol were increased at double the rate of inflation. (The total increase in taxes was around £5 billion, or more than 2% of national income.) Interest rates were cut by 2%, although the cut was reversed later in the year when sterling fell further than had been desired or anticipated.

As expected, the Budget was very unpopular at the time and quite mystifying to economists who still believed in orthodox Keynesian analysis. An unprecedented 364 of these economists published a statement in *The Times* on 30 March 1981, claiming that the government's strategy was misguided [*Doc. 8*]. Here was the ideal time for the 'wets' to hatch a plot against the leadership. However, the nearest they came to a plot appears to have been a breakfast between Prior, Walker and Gilmour on the morning of Budget day. This came to nothing when they realised that Whitelaw, Carrington and Pym, who would be essential allies in a coup, although displeased with the Budget, were not willing to revolt. The Budget was thus a successful demonstration of Mrs Thatcher's resolve to do what she believed in and not to buckle under pressure. For a period after the 1981 Budget this resolve was to be vigorously tested, and not just in economic policy.

When she became Prime Minister, Margaret Thatcher was no stranger to terrorist atrocities perpetrated by Irish nationalists. Only two days after the 1979 election was called her close friend and advisor Airey Neave had been killed by a car bomb in the House of Commons car park, planted by the Irish National Liberation Army (INLA). Once in office the killing continued and 27 August 1979 saw the murder of Lord Mountbatten off the coast at Mullaghmore, County Sligo and the explosion of two bombs at Warrenpoint, near Newry, which killed 18 soldiers. The terrorist outrages were accompanied by a series of 'dirty protests' in prisons, in which Irish Republican Army (IRA) prisoners smeared faeces around their cells. These eventually gave way to the more serious hunger strikes, where prisoners refused to eat until their demands were met. The essential demand of the IRA hunger strikers was for them to be acknowledged as 'political prisoners' rather than simply as criminals, and on 1 March 1981 the IRA leader in the Maze, Bobby Sands, began a hunger strike in support of this cause that was joined by other prisoners. Mrs Thatcher, however, was resolute in her attitude that the strikers were common criminals and there would be absolutely no question of concessions. Bobby Sands duly died on 5 May. Nine more strikers followed him to the grave during the summer until the strike was finally called off on 3 October. The prisoners had failed to secure the political status they demanded and Mrs Thatcher had shown that she would not bow to the moral blackmail of terrorists. She considered the outcome a 'significant defeat for the IRA' [28 *p. 393*], although the hunger strikes brought about a steep rise in support for Sinn Fein, the political arm of the IRA, which had important consequences in the years ahead.

Mrs Thatcher's resolve was to be tested again in the industrial relations field with the onset of the Civil Service strike in March 1981. After the government's humiliation at the hands of the miners in February, it was essential, if Mrs Thatcher's strategy of standing up to the unions was to maintain credibility, that the government did not buckle as the Civil Service strike began to take effect. This time ministers were directly in the firing line in that the government was the employer in the dispute. The unions demanded a 15% pay rise, but the government maintained that only 7% was on offer. Selective strikes took place and the amount lost in unpaid taxes and interest charges on money borrowed to cover delayed tax collection was estimated at £350–500 million. The strike continued for 21 weeks before the unions eventually settled for a 7.5% rise. Mrs Thatcher may have considered that the 'demonstration effect' had been successfully applied though it was not without controversy within her own ranks. In early June it appeared that the unions would have settled for a 7.5% increase, a course advocated by the minister in charge of the Civil Service, Lord Soames, now back from Rhodesia. Mrs Thatcher thought this a sellout, and threatened to resign if the unions were offered more than 7%. The strike thus continued for a further seven weeks, at an estimated cost of £500 million [76 *p. 229*], until Mrs Thatcher agreed that they could be offered the extra money. She thus demonstrated her resolve, but at no small cost.

The area in which Mrs Thatcher's resolve faced the sternest test, however, remained economic policy. April 1981 saw violent riots in London's Brixton and these were repeated in other parts of the country, including Liverpool, as the year continued. Mrs Thatcher's critics claimed that these riots were evidence of the growing social problems that her economic strategy and the ensuing unemployment were generating. Mrs Thatcher vehemently denied such a connection, refusing to accept that unemployment was a main cause of the rioting and instead took steps to ensure the police were given all the support they needed in dealing with the disturbances. Through all these turbulent months of 1981, economic policy was to remain unchanged. But if Mrs Thatcher herself was willing to remain resolute as the economic situation failed to improve, the same cannot be said for all her Cabinet colleagues.

It soon became clear that the January reshuffle had not gone far enough in re-establishing her authority, as the 'wets' continued to oppose vociferously her economic policy. The disagreements came to a head at a Cabinet discussion on economic policy on 23 July. The 'wets' lined up in force to oppose Mrs Thatcher and Howe's monetarist line and even ministers who Mrs Thatcher thought supported her, such as John Nott, counselled against making the further public expenditure cuts that she saw as essential. Mrs Thatcher described the meeting as: 'one of the bitterest arguments on the economy, or any subject, that I can ever recall taking place at Cabinet during my premiership' [28 *p. 148*].

Heavily outnumbered by her opponents, Mrs Thatcher agreed to postpone a decision on the expenditure cuts until later in the year. After this 'wet' victory, leaking and open dissent from the government line continued throughout the summer with Pym and Peter Thorneycroft, the Party Chairman, being notably outspoken in speeches pointing out the lack of success in dealing with the recession. Mrs Thatcher therefore decided to complete the work that she had left unfinished in January with a September reshuffle to purge the Cabinet of the 'wets' who most vociferously opposed her economic prescription.

Gilmour, Soames and Carlisle were simply removed from the government, while Thorneycroft, a long-standing critic of high public spending, lost the post of Party Chairman. Furthermore, Prior, whose attitude towards trade union reform was fundamentally softer than Mrs Thatcher's, was dispatched to the wilderness of the Northern Ireland Office. In place of these 'wets' Mrs Thatcher chose to promote politicians who were to become some of her closest allies over the next few years. These included Nigel Lawson, who was a prime mover in the development of the MTFS, to Energy; Norman Tebbit to Employment; and the youthful Cecil Parkinson to become the new Party Chairman. Keith Joseph, the purest new right philosher within the Cabinet, was moved from the DTI to become Education Secretary. Joseph's spell at the DTI had been surprisingly inglorious from a Thatcherite point of view as he had been forced to authorise increasing subsidies for ailing companies, most notably British Leyland. Although the government's philosophy, much of which had come from Joseph, was to avoid bailing out unprofitable companies threatened with bankruptcy, the loss of jobs that would be associated with British Leyland going bankrupt was deemed politically unacceptable and increased subsidies were thus inevitable. Joseph's move notwithstanding, the crucial part of the 1981 reshuffle was undoubtedly the purge of the 'wets'. Furious to see such an erosion of their power base, they launched one final attack on Mrs Thatcher's policies at a pivotal annual party conference in October. With unemployment still high, and as yet little evidence that monetarism was solving Britain's problems, she was still in an exposed position. Despite the fierce attacks on the government being led by Ted Heath, Mrs Thatcher maintained the confidence of the conference.

As 1981 drew to a close, Mrs Thatcher was thus beginning to feel more in control of her government. By the time of the 1982 Budget, which for the first time was preceded by a pre-Budget Cabinet, public borrowing was below the level forecast and Howe was able to present a relatively bold Budget, cutting taxes but also providing help for industry and jobs. Nevertheless, despite the early signs of economic recovery, the government remained unpopular in the country. However, on 2 April 1982 Argentina invaded the Falkland Islands, the British territory in the South Atlantic. Mrs Thatcher's standing was about to be transformed.

THE FALKLANDS WAR AND ITS AFTERMATH (1981-83)

Britain had claimed sovereignty over the Falkland Islands and had been in continuous occupation of them since 1833, but Argentina, who insisted that sovereignty resided with them, had always rejected this claim. Since the 1970s the Argentinians had stated their claim more forcefully, and the Thatcher government had attempted to address the issue by assigning a junior minister, Nicholas Ridley, to propose a solution. However, after Ridley's plan for returning sovereignty to Argentina (combined with a long-term lease of the islands back to Britain) was savagely attacked in the House of Commons in December 1980, the issue was shelved.

A misjudgement followed with the 1981 Strategic Defence Review when John Nott, who had replaced Pym chiefly because Mrs Thatcher believed he would be more willing than Pym to make cuts, decided to save £3 million by removing *HMS Endurance* from service on the Falklands. With her 20 marines the ship was hardly a viable defence against an aggressor, but the Foreign Office had pointed out that to remove the token defence of the islands might encourage Argentinian aggression, especially given the increasingly hostile rhetoric of General Galtieri, who had seized control of the governing military Junta in December 1981. However, the Foreign Office's advice was overruled by a Defence Secretary determined to make the cuts that the leader expected. It was to prove false economy of the most extreme kind.

The 19 March 1982 saw the Argentinian flag flying on the nearby British dependency of South Georgia. While the Argentine Junta claimed no knowledge of this landing, by the evening of 31 March London was receiving intelligence stating that Argentina would invade the islands on 2 April. The intelligence proved accurate. Mrs Thatcher's response was one of outrage and determination that such aggression could not be allowed to succeed. On 31 March Sir Henry Leach, the Chief of Naval Staff, began to assemble a task force capable of retaking the Islands, and on 2 April the Cabinet gave its approval for the task force to sail. But before the armed forces were put to the test, Mrs Thatcher faced her own test in explaining the whole affair to the House of Commons.

She describes the debate on Saturday 3 April as 'the most difficult I ever had to face' [28 *p. 183*] and it is certainly true that she desperately needed to reassert her authority after the national humiliation that many claimed her government should have predicted and avoided. She faced two tasks in the emergency House of Commons debate, most exceptionally called for a Saturday morning: she had first to defend the government for allowing the crisis to occur, and secondly to ensure the House's backing for decisive action against Argentina. The second proved easier than the first, as the Commons appeared more outraged than Mrs Thatcher [*Doc. 9*] and even Michael Foot, the Labour leader, stated that Britain had a 'moral duty, a political duty and every other sort of duty' to win back the Islands [47 *p. 287*]. But she was less successful in defending the government's track record. The Commons wanted a scapegoat, and after huge pressure from MPs and the media, Mrs Thatcher was forced to accept the resignation of Lord Carrington and two junior Foreign Office ministers.

Although Mrs Thatcher did not want Carrington to resign, there was no doubt that his resignation helped catalyse badly needed party unity and this need for unity drove her to appoint Francis Pym to replace Carrington as Foreign Secretary. In normal circumstances she would not have considered appointing Pym to such a senior post as he was undoubtedly an arch 'wet', but for the moment she had little choice.

Mrs Thatcher needed the support not only of her party, but also now of foreign leaders and the Commonwealth and EC were generally supportive. After some brilliant diplomatic manoeuvring by Britain's UN representative, Anthony Parsons, a resolution of the UN Security Council (UNSCR 502) was soon passed, calling for the immediate and unconditional withdrawal of Argentina from the Falklands. This established a strong basis for Britain's diplomatic campaign and any future military action.

The ally that Mrs Thatcher most needed in the months ahead was the United States. She had high hopes, as in January 1981 Ronald Reagan had been sworn in as US President, and the two leaders had already begun to enjoy a 'special relationship'. Mrs Thatcher had first met Reagan in 1975. Despite their very different styles, they found they not only shared the same philosophy of limited government, but also got on well at a personal level. Mrs Thatcher became the first foreign leader to visit Reagan after his inauguration as President and their close rapport was widely noticed. However, while Britain was the US's long-standing ally, a certain conflict of interest came into play. The South American lobby had a strong voice in Washington and the Reagan administration, keen to retain influence in Buenos Aires, was deeply divided over what line to take. Initially America was able to avoid openly favouring either side, as Secretary of State Al Haig took on the role of mediator. This fell far short of the unconditional support Mrs Thatcher had hoped for. The USA produced various peace plans throughout the conflict, but they only served to illustrate that neither Mrs Thatcher nor Argentina would compromise on the central issues, with Mrs Thatcher demanding British sovereignty over the Falklands and restoration of British rule, but Argentina refusing to withdraw its troops. It was only after the peace initiatives had failed that US policy openly tilted in favour of Britain, although the Pentagon had been quietly helpful from the first, providing the latest air-to-air missiles and vital intelligence.

South Georgia was recaptured on 25 April [*Doc. 10*], but the first serious casualties came with the sinking of the Argentinian cruiser, *General Belgrano*, on 2 May. The *Belgrano* was sighted by the submarine *HMS Conqueror* just outside the exclusion zone announced by the British government, but Mrs Thatcher agreed to a military request to change the rules of engagement to allow the *Belgrano* to be sunk. At the time it was claimed that the *Belgrano* was preparing to attack British ships, although it later transpired that she was sailing away from the task force when sunk. Tam Dalyell MP claimed that the sinking was a political decision designed to scupper the chances of a new peace initiative launched by Peru, but Mrs Thatcher always vigorously denied this, stating that she simply followed the advice of the military who at the time believed the *Belgrano* to be a threat [*Doc. 11*]. Two days later *HMS Sheffield* was sunk, with the loss of 21 lives, and the chances of a diplomatic solution plummeted. Diplomatic activity continued for several weeks more, but the prospects of a peaceful solution had probably never been good. Both sides used diplomacy to shore up international support for their position rather than as a means of reaching an accommodation that neither seriously believed possible.

British troops landed on the Falklands' San Carlos Bay on 21 May, and after a fierce struggle which involved the loss of several more British ships and some hand-to-hand combat, victory was achieved on 14 June with an Argentinian surrender. The Falklands crisis allowed Mrs Thatcher's bold and decisive leadership to be seen in the best possible light, but she was walking a tightrope as victory was by no means assured and defeat would have meant certain resignation. A subsequent committee of enquiry led by the veteran official Lord Franks exonerated Mrs Thatcher's government of any blame for the crisis. Her popularity rating shot up to 51% and the 'Falklands Factor' allowed her to achieve a powerbase she had never before known.

This new-found hegemony did not, however, mean omnipotence. The continuing limitations on her position are illustrated by the incident concerning a paper containing options for social policy, which was published by the Central Policy Review Staff (CPRS) and circulated to Cabinet in September 1982. This paper contained very radical proposals such as ending free health care and was leaked to *The Economist* magazine [*Doc. 12*]. Although Mrs Thatcher claims to have been 'horrified' by the paper [28 *p. 277*], the commentator and her biographer, Hugh Young, has claimed that it had her support and was forced off the agenda by an aghast Cabinet [76 *p. 301*]. The strong reaction against any tinkering with the welfare state helped ward her off radicalism in social policy until her third term.

Radicalism was evident, however, in the government's privatisation policy. Although privatisation had not featured in the 1979 manifesto, by 1983 British Aerospace, Cable and Wireless, Amersham International and Britoil all had at least 50% of their equity in the private sector. Shares in BP had also been sold off as had British Rail's hotels. While the intended flagship privatisation of the first term, British Airways, had been temporarily delayed by litigation by Laker Airways, the privatisation of the first term marked a trend that was set to accelerate during Mrs Thatcher's next term of office.

The 1983 election manifesto was published on 18 May. In addition to accelerating privatisation, it pledged that a second Conservative administration would enact further trade union reforms and reform local government, notably by abolishing the Greater London Council. On 9 May the election was called for one month's time, and as the campaign began opinion polls showed that the Conservatives led Labour by 14% [28 *p. 291*]. The 1983 Labour manifesto, famously described by Gerald Kaufman as 'the longest suicide note in history', was to many of the electorate unacceptably left-wing. This played into Mrs Thatcher's hands and the Conservatives dominated the campaign, wining a majority of 144, the largest since 1945, despite securing just 42.4% of the popular vote.

This victory was seen by Thatcherites as an approval of Mrs Thatcher's record and a mandate for more of the same. To those who claimed her victory was simply due to the windfall benefits of the successful conclusion to the Falklands War, her defenders stressed that even before the war the popularity of her government was increasing as the economic reforms began to bring results. Furthermore, by election year there were definite signs of economic recovery, with output growing by 4% and consumer spending rising. In reality, her 144 majority was not the electorate giving her economic record the seal of approval, but neither was it simply the 'Falklands Factor'. Her victory was due to a number of favourable circumstances, including the above two, although another of great significance was the dire state of the opposition.

Since the election in 1979 the extreme left had attempted to win control of the Labour Party. In 1980 they ensured the election of the radical Michael Foot, rather than the more mainstream Denis Healey, to succeed Callaghan as leader. The Labour moderates then split from the main Labour Party with the 'Gang of Four' – David Owen, Shirley Williams, Bill Rodgers and Roy Jenkins – forming the Social Democratic Party in March 1981. The result of this split was a double bonus for Mrs Thatcher as not only was opposition to her divided, thus making a Conservative defeat more difficult, but Labour's policies after the breakaway became even more extreme, losing them support. Michael Foot himself compounded the problem as even Roy Hattersley admitted that 'it was difficult to find anyone who regarded him as a credible candidate for the office of Prime Minister' [47 *p. 293*].

The 1983 election victory was thus the result of a lucky combination of factors, of which only one was admiration for Mrs Thatcher's leadership. The late Peter Jenkins further argued that the election result illustrated Mrs Thatcher's success in changing the attitudes of the electorate: at least in economic terms the country 'lowered its expectations' [52 *p. 153*] and was willing to accept that problems, such as the massive levels of unemployment, were not the fault of the government [*Doc. 13*]. Whatever the causes of her victory, however, what cannot be doubted is that after the election Mrs Thatcher's position was well established and her survival as Prime Minister, at least for the foreseeable future, was assured.

3 THE HIGH TIDE OF THATCHER

A TROUBLED START (1983)

Despite the mandate given to Mrs Thatcher with her massive 144 majority in the 1983 general election, she was unable to ensure that her second administration began with the conviction and energy she hoped for, as a series of embarrassments was to buffet the government. These problems were to help her second term earn the unwelcome name, 'The Parliament of Banana Skins' [14 p. 271].

The slow start may be partly explained by the 1983 manifesto. Mrs Thatcher acknowledges that it failed to inspire a 'crusading spirit' as it simply promised 'more of the same' [28 p. 305], a fact reflected in the 1983 Queen's Speech, described by The Times as having 'no radical edge' [4 23.6.83]. However there was certainly plenty of legislation promised, and Mrs Thatcher was particularly keen to build upon the radicalism of her first term in trade union reform and privatisation. With the boost to her authority and confidence from her landslide majority, she at last felt able to appoint a strongly Thatcherite Cabinet which might, she hoped, relegate struggles over policy to the past.

Early reshuffles

Her resolve is well demonstrated by her decision to ask Francis Pym, the Foreign Secretary, to leave the Cabinet. Mrs Thatcher had never been fond of Pym, who had been appointed largely for the sake of party unity during the Falklands crisis. He had not impressed her since and had probably sealed his fate by explaining, on the BBC's Question Time programme during the campaign, that landslide majorities did not necessarily produce good government. Mrs Thatcher and Pym simply did not get on: 'Francis and I disagreed on the direction of policy, in our approach to government and indeed about life in general' [28 p. 306].

To replace him, Mrs Thatcher moved Geoffrey Howe from the Treasury and Nigel Lawson, the Energy Secretary, became Chancellor.

Lawson was one of the most brilliant exponents of Thatcherite economics, had so far shown nothing but loyalty to the leader and was thus an ideal candidate to keep her economic strategy on course. William Whitelaw was also moved. Although Mrs Thatcher claims that he had become 'indispensable' [28 *p. 307*] in Cabinet, he did not share her hard-line views on Home Office matters, disagreeing with her for example over capital punishment. He thus became Leader of the House of Lords and Leon Brittan became Home Secretary. Brittan was a 'complete Thatcher creation' [76 *p. 335*] as his meteoric rise to the Cabinet and now the Home Office was entirely her personal decision. Realising this, he was unquestionably loyal. For the first time in her premiership, the three great offices of state (Exchequer, Foreign Office, Home Office) were occupied by ideological Thatcherites. However, her appointees were not to remain forever the loyal Thatcherites that she believed them to be when promoting them.

'Banana skins' now began to appear in her pathway with monotonous regularity. She had been planning to make the Party Chairman, Cecil Parkinson, who had organised a very efficient and effective election campaign, Foreign Secretary. However her problems began on the day after the 1983 election when Mrs Thatcher learned that Parkinson had made his secretary, Sara Keays, pregnant. Nevertheless, Mrs Thatcher still wanted his loyal support in Cabinet and he was therefore sent to the less high-profile Department of Trade and Industry (DTI). But it was not low profile enough. After the affair became public, in October 1983, even Mrs Thatcher's support was not enough to save him. In Parkinson's eyes, the press were 'in the grip of collective hysteria' [24 *p. 250*] and having been denounced by Keays, he was forced to resign.

The economy soon provided a second 'banana skin'. Despite a rise in economic optimism before the election, when it seemed that a recovery had begun, soon after the election the state of the economy worsened considerably. With inflation and unemployment rising, interest rates had to be increased by 1.5% and public borrowing looked set to be £3 billion higher than earlier Treasury forecasts. Lawson therefore had to assemble an emergency package to help bring the PSBR down. This package reduced the deficit by £1 billion, half of which came from the sale of BP (British Petroleum) shares but the rest came from genuine public expenditure cuts. Lawson acknowledges that having to make such cuts so soon after a General Election was 'embarrassing' [23 *p. 283*] as opponents could argue that by postponing painful cuts until after they were safely elected, the government had been dishonest with the electorate.

The invasion of Grenada

Another embarrassment occurred in the former British colony of Grenada, over 6,000 kilometres away in the Caribbean Sea. The problems began when, on 19 October, Maurice Bishop, Grenada's Marxist leader, was deposed and murdered by a more extreme left-wing group. The United States claimed a special interest in the problem and on 25 October American soldiers invaded Grenada, capturing the coup leaders and ending the Communist regime.

This left Mrs Thatcher's government with a true dilemma. Grenada was a member of the Commonwealth and the Queen was the Head of State, but Britain's supposed closest ally had made no serious attempt to take the views of the British government into account before deciding to invade. As soon as Reagan told her of his intention, Mrs Thatcher immediately communicated her deep reservations, but while she may have given Reagan 'a prime ticking off' [74 p. 210] [Doc. 14], she was unable to persuade him to abandon the intervention. The government's humiliating lack of influence in Washington was made especially painful as the day before the invasion Howe had answered a question in the Commons, asking whether or not America would intervene, by saying: 'I know of no such intention' [21 p. 328].

Despite this, Mrs Thatcher believed Britain's friendship with the United States 'must on no account be jeopardised' [28 p. 333] and the incident was 'not allowed by either side permanently to sour Anglo-American relations, despite the humiliation and associated difficulties it caused for the Thatcher government.

VINTAGE THATCHER (1984–85)

Although the second term may have started badly, in the early part of this term Mrs Thatcher did achieve several objectives that were most important to her mission. Three accomplishments in particular stand out: increasing momentum for privatisation, an EC budget settlement and the defeat of the NUM.

Privatisation

Privatisation was a crucial ingredient of Thatcherism. She argued that whereas nationalised companies were controlled by politicians and the civil service, the widespread share ownership resulting from privatisation left companies under the control of many individuals – 'the state's power is reduced and the power of the people enhanced' [28 p. 676]. The government's coffers were the welcome beneficiaries of these sales of assets to the private sector. Privatisation moreover could be justified on grounds of economic efficiency as nationalised companies, being supported by the state, had little chance of going bankrupt and thus little motivation to ensure they operated efficiently. Such an all out attack on the 'mixed' economy, in contrast to the toleration and, indeed, support of nationalisation by all her postwar predecessors as Tory leader, marked Mrs Thatcher out very clearly. None were the free market, capitalist supporter that she was and Harold Macmillan, Conservative Prime Minister (1957–63), lambasted the government for 'selling the family silver' [16 *p. 95*].

While some privatisation had occurred during her first term, only relatively smaller companies (British Aerospace, Cable and Wireless, Amersham International, Britoil and Associated British Ports) had been privatised, some only partially. These achievements were to be dwarfed by what was to follow. In June 1984, Enterprise Oil was floated on the stock exchange and this was followed by Jaguar in July. The most significant privatisation to date, however, was British Telecom, which had 50.2% of its equity sold in November 1984, raising £3,916 million. This was significant as British Telecom was the first public utility to be sold and it raised far more than all the previous sales put together. The privatisation bandwagon was now given a tremendous push: British Gas was sold in 1986, and British Airways and Rolls Royce before the election in 1987. 'Popular' capitalism had become the vogue: now the 'ordinary' British voter could own not just his house, but also shares: a revolution was seen to be underway and was set to continue throughout Mrs Thatcher's time in office.

An EC budget settlement

The second early achievement of her third term was a settlement of Britain's contribution to the EC budget, still declared excessive even after Mrs Thatcher's stance in 1979–80. She was determined to achieve a permanent settlement that 'would last as long as the problem would last' [21 *p. 399*]. In this quest, she was helped by the fact that the leaders representing both France and Germany had changed since she had last fought for a settlement: Germany's Schmidt had been replaced by Helmut Kohl and France's Giscard d'Estaing by François Mitterrand. Although she never enjoyed a very warm personal relationship with either of these leaders, her relationship with them was certainly less difficult than her relationship with their predecessors, and this enhanced the chances of a settlement. However, despite the decrease in personal enmity, at summits her style remained as abrasive and stubborn as ever.

Both the Stuttgart Summit in June 1983 and the Athens Summit that December were deadlocked as Mrs Thatcher refused to co-operate with her fellow EC leaders until the budget issue was resolved. The Athens Summit ended, for the first time in the EC's history, without a communiqué. The Brussels Summit of March 1984 fared little better as Mrs Thatcher chose to reject an offer of a 1,000 million ECU (European Currency Unit) rebate for five years on the familiar grounds that she would settle for nothing less than a permanent solution. Her permanent solution was finally found at the Fontainebleau Summit (June 1984), under the Presidency of Mitterrand. The leaders managed to agree a formula that would result in a fixed percentage refund of the difference between the money Britain paid in and the money paid out by the EC. The fiercest argument, however, came in deciding what percentage the refund would take. Mrs Thatcher wanted over 70% while the other leaders suggested around 50%, but after much hard bargaining a figure of 66% (two thirds) was agreed. Mrs Thatcher therefore had a settlement along her own lines, and while some commentators such as Hugo Young have suggested that a less confrontational approach could have brought agreement sooner [76 *p. 383*], Mrs Thatcher continued to believe that reaching the agreement vindicated her aggressive style of diplomacy.

With the budget issue resolved, Britain worked hard to promote the idea of a single market across the EC. Indeed, by adopting the single market idea as her principal European initiative, Mrs Thatcher's image of hostility towards the EC was softened considerably. Her efforts bore fruit when the EC leaders agreed, at the Luxembourg EC Summit of December 1985, what was to become the Single European Act (SEA), providing for the completion of the European single market. However, in its extension of qualified majority voting in the Council of Ministers (unless a vital national interest was at stake) and its pledge to 'ensure the convergence of economic and monetary policies' within the EC [*Doc. 15*], the Act prepared for European integration far beyond a single market. By agreeing the SEA, Mrs Thatcher herself thus helped progress towards the European integration which she was to denounce so strongly during her third term.

Industrial relations and the miners' strike

The greatest struggle of the second term was to come in industrial relations. Confirmation of Mrs Thatcher's continuing hostility to the unions came on 25 January 1984 with Foreign Secretary Howe's announcement of a ban on trade unions at the highly security sensitive Government Communications Headquarters (GCHQ). GCHQ was based in Cheltenham and was responsible for intelligence gathering by eavesdropping Soviet and other foreign governments' communications.

With 10,000 working days lost at GCHQ between 1979 and 1981 through protests [21 *p. 339*], the government justified the ban on unions on the grounds of national security, as further strikes could threaten the accumulation of vital intelligence.

Howe's announcement was unexpected and both the opposition and the trade union movement were outraged: even some Conservatives thought that the government had gone too far. There may have been a good cause for the government's action, but the episode was managed in a high-handed way [*Doc. 16*]. In the House of Commons, Denis Healey's response to Howe's announcement laid the blame with Mrs Thatcher, calling her 'the Mephistopheles' behind Howe's 'shabby Faust': 'Her pig-headed bigotry has prevented her closest colleagues and Sir Robert Armstrong [Cabinet Secretary] from offering and accepting a compromise' [19 *p. 506*].

Healey's criticism was not wide of the mark as Robert Armstrong and others had proposed an alternative scheme to an absolute ban on unions, consisting of allowing them to exist but banning industrial action. Mrs Thatcher, however, would not back down, claiming that employees would always face a conflict of loyalty between their trade union and their employer, and the work at GCHQ was too sensitive to allow this conflict to exist. Her resolve hardened once the announcement was made public with her Chief Press Secretary, Bernard Ingham, an increasingly influential advisor, pointing out that any flexibility on her part would be seen as a U-turn [22 *p. 236*]. The incident certainly demonstrated Mrs Thatcher's absolute refusal to bow to trade union pressure, but this resolve was about to face its toughest test: GCHQ was merely the prelude.

When Margaret Thatcher came to power in 1979, memories of the trade unions' part in bringing down the government of Edward Heath in February 1974 had far from faded. Furthermore, Mrs Thatcher's attempts to ensure that trade union pressure could not override the demands of economic efficiency had already been thwarted by the National Union of Mineworkers (NUM) when the threat of a strike forced a government climb down in 1981. This action appeared to suggest that, faced with the powerful coal industry, Mrs Thatcher's government was just as powerless as Heath's (and Labour's) had been. When the new far-left leader of the NUM, Arthur Scargill, declared that with the new Thatcher government's large majority 'extra-parliamentary action will be the only course open to the working class and the labour movement' [76 *p. 367*], confrontation looked increasingly likely. Mrs Thatcher, however, was determined to prove that it was she and not the NUM that ruled Britain. Since the 1981 defeat she had realised that, to beat the NUM, the government would have to survive a long strike, and ensuring that this could be done successfully had necessitated extensive preparations.

As Energy Secretary, Nigel Lawson produced detailed plans ensuring that stockpiles of coal at power stations were discreetly increased to allow the continued generation of power during a coal strike. Lawson's plans even went as far as to identify potential helicopter landing sites at the power stations so that chemicals that were necessary in addition to coal could be flown in. The government also made sure that the police were fully equipped and trained to deal with any violence that might develop at pickets as striking miners attempted to stop others working.

Mrs Thatcher's determination to reform the coal industry was strengthened by a 1983 Monopolies and Mergers Commission report that suggested that 75% of coal mines were making a loss. Mrs Thatcher's attitude was that so-called 'uneconomic pits' would have to close. In September 1983, the hard-nosed American industrialist, Ian MacGregor, was appointed with a mission of bringing the industry to profit, an objective that he had fulfilled in Britain's steel industry with resultant heavy job losses. Scargill's attitude to 'uneconomic pits' was simple: they did not exist. The only justification for closing a pit was that there was no more coal left to extract. Confrontation became inevitable [Doc. 17].

The confrontation began on 1 March 1984 with a local announcement that the Cortonwood Colliery was to close. Five days later MacGregor announced plans to close another 20 'uneconomic' pits. The strike began on 12 March, but it became clear that Scargill had run into two particular problems. First, he had begun the struggle in the spring so that the strikers would have to endure a summer without wages, while the demand for coal would remain low. Secondly, he did not call a national strike ballot. He had lost three ballots since becoming leader of the NUM, the most recent being in March 1983, and he feared that in those pits where miners received good pay and there was little chance of closure, there would be little enthusiasm for strike action. There was thus no guarantee of a national endorsement of a nationwide strike. Therefore instead of a formal national strike, Scargill attempted to build up a combination of regional strikes that would have the same effect. Even with the use of violent secondary pickets, however, he was unable to close down the entire mining industry. Pits in Nottinghamshire, Warwickshire and Leicestershire continued to work, and lorry drivers were willing to risk the hostile pickets to get coal to the power stations.

The government tried to insist publicly that the dispute was between the NUM and the National Coal Board (NCB) and that it was not the government's role to intervene, but in her memoirs Mrs Thatcher admits that she considered the conflict to be so serious that it required discreet government intervention. An example of this intervention came after the National Association of Colliery Overmen, Deputies and Shotfirers (NACODS) voted to strike on 28 September. Such a strike would have been disastrous as health and safety regulations required that a qualified supervisor (most of whom were members of NACODS) had to be present if coal were to be mined. A NACODS strike thus had the potential to shut down the remaining pits and end the supplies that were keeping the power stations running. The government therefore put pressure on MacGregor to produce an acceptable settlement, which he did, and on 24 October the NACODS agreed not to strike. The battle was not going the NUM's way. On 25 October the NUM had its funds sequestrated after refusing to pay a £200,000 fine for contempt of court. This was the first in a series of massive legal defeats for the union at the hands of the new trade union legislation, with the 1980 and 1982 Acts now supplemented by the 1984 Trade Union Act that required a strike ballot to be held if a union was to enjoy legal immunity. After a mild winter in 1984–85 it became clear that the miners were failing to cripple the country as they had done in the days of the Heath government. By mid-January 1985, 2,500 demoralised miners were returning to work every week and NUM delegates voted formally to end the strike on 3 March.

Although the strike had cost the country over £2 billion, Lawson believed that 'it was necessary that the government spent whatever was necessary to defeat Arthur Scargill' [23 *pp. 160–1*]. The government had wanted to exorcise the myth, present since the defeat of Heath, that ultimately even a democratically elected government could not govern without the support of the NUM. This had been shown to be false and thus for pro-Thatcher commentators such as Martin Holmes, the defeat of the NUM was 'the single most important event in the course of the Parliament to further Thatcherism' [51 *p. 154*]. To Mrs Thatcher, herself, it had established that 'Britain could not be made ungovernable by the Fascist Left' [28 *p. 378*].

Ironically, although polls had revealed the public to be strongly anti-Scargill, his defeat did not bring the improvement in the low Conservative poll ratings that some ministers such as Norman Tebbit thought was deserved [27 *p. 238*]. Worse, Mrs Thatcher's government was about to enter a phase of mid-term difficulties.

MID-TERM DIFFICULTIES (1985–86)

The government's difficulties became evident when, just over two months after defeating the NUM, the local government elections of May 1985 saw heavy Tory losses. Francis Pym seized this moment to attempt to form a group within the Conservative Party that was opposed to Mrs Thatcher's right-wing policies. Although 'Centre Forward', as the group was called, failed to attract any significant open support and was 'immediately judged a pathetic failure' [76 *p. 495*], backbenchers remained very uneasy with the government's performance. Morale fell still further when the 4 July Brecon and Radnor by-election saw the Liberals take the previously Conservative seat with a swing of 16%.

Mrs Thatcher believed that the government's problem was 'presentation and therefore personnel' [28 *p. 417*] rather than policy, and a Cabinet reshuffle followed on 2 September. The major change was Douglas Hurd's replacement of Leon Brittan as Home Secretary as Mrs Thatcher claimed that Brittan 'just did not carry conviction with the public' [28 *p. 419*]. He was given the lesser but still important job of heading the DTI: the Home Office thus lost a true Thatcherite and gained a 'One Nation' Tory. Other core changes included the replacement of John Gummer, who had not impressed Mrs Thatcher as Party Chairman, by Norman Tebbit, a true Thatcherite believer, with orders to prepare the party for the next general election. An attempt was also made to improve presentation at the Department of the Environment by replacing Patrick Jenkin with Kenneth Baker. This reshuffle was well received by the demoralised party, but it soon became clear that the nadir of the second term was far from over.

The Anglo-Irish Agreement

One area in which the government appeared to be successfully taking the initiative was Irish policy. The Anglo-Irish Agreement was signed on 15 November 1985, but discussions between the British and Irish governments, with a view to improving security in Northern Ireland, had been taking place since early in the second term. These discussions were slow and broke off completely after the IRA bombed the Grand Hotel at Brighton on 12 October 1984. The entire Conservative Cabinet was staying there during the Party Conference and the bomb was clearly intended to murder the Prime Minister. Mrs Thatcher survived unscathed, but five people were killed and Norman Tebbit and John Wakeham, two of her closest ministers, were seriously injured. The negotiations with the Irish were broken off as she was determined to avoid any charge of negotiating under duress.

When an agreement finally emerged, Mrs Thatcher trumpeted the fact that the Republic of Ireland had accepted in an international treaty that there could be no change in the status of Northern Ireland without the consent of a majority of its inhabitants. She also hoped that the agreement would lead to more co-operation between the Royal Ulster Constabulary (RUC) and the Irish Police, thus improving security. Unionists, however, saw it as a 'substantial step towards the all-Ireland solution' [47 *p. 330*] and were outraged that the agreement gave the South a consultative role in governing the North [*Doc. 18*]. Ian Gow, now a junior Treasury minister, but who during the first term had built up a reputation as 'the most powerful man in government' [13 *p. 122*] due to his close relationship with Mrs Thatcher while her Parliamentary Private Secretary (PPS), shared the Unionist view that it was nothing short of betrayal and resigned. To this personal blow was added political embarrassment as all 15 Unionist MPs resigned their seats in protest and there followed strikes in Northern Ireland. There was little evidence that the agreement brought the improvements in security that had been hoped for. However, the agreement was a bold and imaginative step for Mrs Thatcher, who in her first term had shown, over the hunger strikes, little willingness to engage in dialogue over the future of Ulster. Her principal lieutenant in negotiating with the Irish, Foreign Secretary Howe, claims that since 1985 the agreement 'has remained the cornerstone of good relations between London and Dublin' [21 *p. 426*]. Nevertheless, Mrs Thatcher now regards the outcome of the agreement as 'disappointing', claiming that too little security co-operation was achieved to merit alienating the Unionists [28 *p. 415*]. However, the political difficulties that Mrs Thatcher experienced as a consequence of the Anglo-Irish Agreement were minimal in comparison with the problems now brewing in domestic politics.

The Westland Affair

The most serious domestic crisis of Mrs Thatcher's premiership until her eventual downfall began over the unlikely case of a disagreement over the future of the Westland Helicopter Company. Westland was the only UK company to produce helicopters but was in danger of going into receivership (bankruptcy). When Michael Heseltine, the Defence Secretary, learned that the Westland Board of Directors was looking favourably upon a rescue package by the American firm, Sikorsky, he declared that it would be better to have a European rescue. Mrs Thatcher, however, backed the view of her DTI Secretary, Leon Brittan, that it was a matter for the Westland Board and did not require government interference. Heseltine, both a pro-European and an interventionist, had different ideas. He personally built up a European rescue package and even persuaded the National Armaments Directors (NADs) of the UK, France, Germany and Italy to agree to buy only European helicopters, thus suggesting that if the Sikorsky bid succeeded, Westland would receive no orders from the NADs' countries. Heseltine had clearly gone against the government's policy of non-interference, turning the issue into a 'full blown political crisis' [42 *p. 278*].

After a meeting of the Cabinet economic committee on Monday 9 December, Heseltine was given until Friday to produce a European bid that would secure the backing of the Westland Board, or else the NADs declaration would be overruled. He claimed that Mrs Thatcher had agreed to a further meeting to discuss his progress, but even when he succeeded in producing a European bid, no such meeting was scheduled. Mrs Thatcher claimed that she had not agreed to a further meeting, but Heseltine asserted that she cancelled the meeting fearing that he had gained the support of his colleagues. Heseltine's conspiracy claims were compounded when Mrs Thatcher refused to have a discussion when he raised the issue without prior warning at Cabinet on 12 December. This exchange ended in 'cold anger on both sides' [12 *p. 302*] and his protest at her decision was not recorded in the Cabinet minutes, despite his request that it should be.

On 13 December, the Westland Board rejected the European bid and three days later, in the House of Commons, Brittan announced the government's policy of neutrality between the two offers: it was a matter for the Board alone. Heseltine had the bit between his teeth, and now refused to accept defeat. Over the Christmas break, he openly flouted the government's collective decision by lobbying for the European bid. After Mrs Thatcher wrote to the Board to make clear that the Sikorsky bid would not harm European contracts, Heseltine sent a letter to Lloyds Bank, which was backing the European Consortium, expressing his view that it would be damaging. Mrs Thatcher then suggested that Heseltine's letter should be referred to the Solicitor-General, Sir Patrick Mayhew, who believed that on the information available to him Heseltine's letter contained 'material inaccuracies'. Mayhew wrote to inform Heseltine of this and on 6 January, selected bits of Mayhew's confidential letter were leaked to the Press Association, severely damaging Heseltine's credibility. The final scene in this extraordinarily bloated political drama came when Mrs Thatcher announced at Cabinet on 9 January that all future statements on Westland would have to be cleared with the Cabinet Office: Heseltine would have to accept the official line. At this, he closed his folder and announced he would have to resign from the Cabinet. He then walked out of Cabinet into a barrage of cameras in the street outside.

That very afternoon he published a statement alleging that he had been denied his right to a full discussion in Cabinet on Westland and that Mrs Thatcher had thus ignored the constitutional principle of collective responsibility. Mrs Thatcher's supporters retorted that Heseltine had used Westland as an excuse to resign from a government in which he knew further promotion was unlikely. He resigned not because he had been denied a constitutional right, but because his views had no support in Cabinet and he 'left a Cabinet united against him' [28 *p. 432*]. Whatever the real reasons for Heseltine's actions it was the way the crisis had been handled that attracted the most criticism, in particular the selective leaking of a confidential law officer's letter.

During the ensuing enquiry, Leon Brittan admitted to authorising the leak, although in later years he claimed to have received 'express permission' from Mrs Thatcher's Chief Press Secretary, Bernard Ingham, and Charles Powell, her foreign affairs private secretary [42 *p. 284*] [*Docs 19 and 20*]. This admission at the time would have explicitly tarred Mrs Thatcher, and Lawson believed that: 'Had [Brittan] made public all he knew, she could not have possibly survived' [23 *p. 679*].

The constitutional issues now moved firmly under the spotlight: Heseltine's resignation, still less the pros and cons of helicopter bids, moved into the background. Mrs Thatcher claimed innocence and ignorance of the leak in the Commons debate on 23 January [*Doc. 21*], and it became clear that Brittan was to be the scapegoat. He accepted this, resigning the next day. Mrs Thatcher defended herself again in the Commons on 27 January and Neil Kinnock spectacularly failed to pin her down to the difficult questions, thus missing the greatest chance to destroy a Conservative PM that he enjoyed as Labour leader. The debate proved decisive and Alan Clark MP's diary recognises Mrs Thatcher's success: 'A brilliant performance, shameless and brave. We are out of the wood' [13 *p. 135*] [*Doc. 22*]. Mrs Thatcher may have survived, but her authority and that of the government was badly damaged. Worse, further humiliations were to follow.

US relations

The anti-American feeling that had surfaced during the Westland Affair returned when the government attempted to sell the major British car manufacturer, British Leyland, to the American company, General Motors (GM). John Wakeham, the Chief Whip, said that he could not promise a majority in the Commons for the government proposals if Land Rover, a subsidiary of Leyland, was included in the sale. Conservative MPs wanted the distinctly British Land Rover to remain British: in the words of Peter Jenkins, it 'touched a chauvinistic nerve' [52 p. 207]. However GM would not agree the deal without Land Rover and thus the sale was abandoned.

On 14 April the government was actually defeated in the Commons when 68 Conservatives rebelled and voted against the Sunday Trading Bill. The month also saw Mrs Thatcher giving Reagan permission to use US aircraft based in Britain for a strike against Libya. This was a response to recent Libyan-sponsored terrorism, in particular a bomb attack in West Berlin on 5 April, resulting in two deaths and some 200 injured. However, as well as hitting military targets, the raids resulted in civilian casualties and received widespread condemnation: a MORI poll showed that 71% of Britons thought that Mrs Thatcher had been wrong to give Reagan permission [4 17.4.86]. On 8 May, the Conservatives suffered two by-election humiliations: in Ryedale the Alliance took the seat, wiping out the 12,000 Tory majority, and in West Derbyshire the Conservative majority was reduced from 15,000 to 100.

While support for Reagan over Libya may have been unpopular, it was part of a policy that Mrs Thatcher saw as very much in Britain's interest: a close relationship with the United States. During the second term, leaving aside the Grenada disagreement, Mrs Thatcher's influence in Washington had bolstered her image as an international stateswoman giving Britain a leading role on the world stage.

The international stateswoman image was born in December 1984 when, three months before he became Soviet Premier, Mikhail Gorbachev met Mrs Thatcher at the PM's country retreat, Chequers. Mrs Thatcher found Gorbachev, unlike other Communists, ready to debate rather than simply read from a prepared brief, and famously announced after the meeting that she 'could do business with Mr Gorbachev' [64 p. 487]. However, she was left in no doubt of Russia's distrust of Reagan's decision to pursue the Strategic Defence Initiative (SDI), which aimed to used a space-based system to destroy incoming ballistic missiles and thus shield America from nuclear attack. This meeting strengthened her fear that SDI could destroy the credibility of nuclear deterrence that had prevented major conflict since 1945. Mrs Thatcher believed that peace was better achieved by a balance of terror than through total nuclear disarmament. Therefore in November she took these fears to Reagan and persuaded him to agree to a statement stressing that SDI was simply a means of enhancing nuclear deterrence rather than achieving Reagan's dream of rendering nuclear weapons obsolete. This outcome helped establish her success in mediating between Washington and Moscow, but also crucially allowed her to demonstrate that the USA and the UK remained united over defence policy. As she stated in Washington: 'There was no question of the Soviet Union being able to divide the United Kingdom from the United States' [76 *p. 399*].

Furthermore, after Reagan came close to undermining the credibility of NATO's nuclear deterrent by almost pledging to scrap all US strategic nuclear weapons at the 1986 Reykjavik Summit with Mikhail Gorbachev, Mrs Thatcher visited Reagan and persuaded him to reaffirm his commitment to a credible nuclear deterrent. One of Reagan's advisors claimed she had prevented an 'utter disaster' [76 *p. 480*]. However, valuable though her role as international mediator and close ally of the US President was, it was of itself to help little in the recovery from the nadir of April 1986.

THE RECOVERY (1986–87)

The Commonwealth
With the continuing difficulties of her second term, Mrs Thatcher's ability as leader had inevitably been called into question. To recover from her nadir she needed an opportunity to reassert strong leadership. One step up came at the special London Commonwealth Summit on South Africa in August 1986.

At the 1985 Commonwealth Heads of Government Meeting in Nassau, Mrs Thatcher had earned the condemnation of the Commonwealth by resisting their demands for economic sanctions on South Africa which were called for as the only way to force South Africa to end apartheid. While Mrs Thatcher 'hated apartheid' [22 *p. 276*], she claimed that sanctions would not end it and would simply cost thousands of black workers their jobs. Despite intense pressure at Nassau she only agreed to a ban on the import of Gold Krugerrands and the ending of government assistance for trade delegations. The sending of an 'Eminent Persons Group' to South Africa was also agreed and it was to be this group's conclusion that economic sanctions were indeed necessary that led to the London Summit. Although she finally conceded support for the EC import ban on South African coal, iron and steel, this fell far short of what the Commonwealth countries demanded, and her intransigence at the summit was condemned by many of their leaders [*Doc. 23*]. Whether or not her opposition to the Commonwealth allowed her to align herself with 'latent racialism at home' [76 *p. 484*] as Hugo Young suggests, or whether, in Bernard

Ingham's words, it was a 'display of political courage and resolution' [22 *p. 279*], it was helpful to Mrs Thatcher in demonstrating her capacity for strong leadership even when she was in a minority of one. However, as she knew well, this was only the very beginning of the Conservative rehabilitation.

Economic upturn

In May 1986, the retirement of her deeply admired but ministerially ineffective mentor, Keith Joseph, allowed her to engineer a modest reshuffle. But the real recovery began only with the October annual party conference. Tebbit's chairmanship of the party was yielding fruit, as 'after months of planning' [27 *p. 252*] the conference was seen as a successful demonstration of party unity [4 *11.10.86*]. Mrs Thatcher believed that it 'set us on course for winning the next election' [28 *p. 567*] and her speech was particularly significant as it highlighted the most significant factor in securing an election victory: economic prosperity.

Economic recovery had been underway throughout the second term, but was becoming increasingly evident as 1986 drew to a close. Inflation stood at 3%, unemployment had peaked at 3.4 million in January 1986 and had fallen ever since, and by June 1987 average weekly earnings had risen by 14% in real terms since the 1983 election. Furthermore, the economic improvement had allowed Chancellor Lawson to ensure that the increasing prosperity was felt, at least by potential Conservative voters.

It is argued that pure monetarism, which claimed that inflation would be brought down simply by adhering to declared targets for monetary growth, was effectively abandoned by Lawson in his 1985 Mansion House Speech. Formal targets for the growth of the £M3 monetary aggregate were discarded and monetary policy looked increasingly towards maintaining exchange rate stability. Furthermore, in his Autumn Statement of November 1986, Lawson announced over £5 billion of additional public expenditure on education, health and housing. This took many commentators by surprise as it came from a government that had previously been desperate to cut government spending. Although Lawson justified the increases by stating that the government's objective was no longer a cut in public expenditure in real cash terms but a cut in the percentage of faster growing GDP, Peter Jenkins claims that 'politics took over from economics ... a last nail in the coffin for monetarism' [52 *pp. 280–1*]. For critics, the decision to increase public expenditure came conveniently close to the general election. Even closer to the election was the 1987

Budget. Here, with a budget surplus of £16 billion, Lawson managed to take 2p off the basic rate of income tax and have no increases in duties on cigarettes and alcohol, thus ensuring the Budget would be popular with the public, but avoided the charge of imprudence and blatant electioneering by showing that the PSBR would still be reduced by £3 billion more than had been originally planned. Lawson could not have done much more to boost the chances of a Conservative victory and all attention now turned to the election campaign.

The general election
The election date of 11 June was announced on 11 May. Eight days later the Conservative manifesto, containing radical proposals for reforms in education, housing, local government finance and trade unions, and the aim of a 25p basic rate of income tax, was launched. Mrs Thatcher regarded it as 'the best ever produced by the Conservative Party' [28 *p. 572*] but the same could not be said of the following election campaign.

As the Conservatives entered the campaign they were faced with two main opponents, Labour and the SDP–Liberal Alliance. Early on, the Tories attacked the Alliance, claiming both that they were socialists in disguise and that they would never win an outright majority – voting for the Alliance would just let Labour in. For the Alliance's part, mutual distrust between their two leaders, David Owen and David Steel, precluded an effective campaign and in the end their support collapsed. However Labour posed more of a threat, and started the campaign well with a professional Party Political Broadcast focusing on Neil Kinnock, party leader since October 1983, which increased his popularity considerably. By contrast the Conservative campaign almost failed to start at all, and Lawson described it as 'the most incompetent in which I have ever participated' [23 *p. 695*].

Mrs Thatcher felt uneasy about Tebbit's growing popularity and independence, and therefore appointed David Young, one of her favourites, to Central Office to keep an eye on him. Through continued disagreement, Tebbit and Young earned the name of 'Margaret's squabbling seconds' [21 *p. 528*], and they even employed rival advertising agencies to produce election material. Despite this background noise, the Conservatives did manage to exploit Labour's unilateral nuclear disarmament policy and through a meticulous costing of Labour's pledges, Lawson forced Kinnock to admit that his claim, that no one earning under £25,000 a year would pay more tax under a Labour government, was wrong.

However, the Conservatives remained uncertain of a secure victory and one week before the election, 'Wobbly Thursday', an opinion poll was published suggesting that the Conservative lead had been cut to 4%. This shook Mrs Thatcher and she persuaded Tebbit to saturate the press with advertisements designed by one of her favourites from the PR world, Tim Bell, at a cost of some £2 million. Although the poll of that Thursday turned out to be inaccurate and poll ratings scarcely changed throughout the campaign, it was only when all the votes had been counted that Mrs Thatcher felt she could relax. She had won another triumph with a majority of 101 and the world lay before her.

4 THE CENTRE CANNOT HOLD

THE REVOLUTION CONTINUES (1987–89)

Although Mrs Thatcher's new majority was reduced by 43 to 101, it was still the largest since 1945, with the exception of her own 1983 landslide. She therefore could be forgiven for thinking that the troubles of the second term had been exorcised and that she had been given a fresh mandate to implement the undoubtedly radical policies that had featured in the 1987 manifesto.

Although the post-election reshuffle was limited, it did allow Mrs Thatcher to produce a Cabinet that demonstrated that she was in charge. Her most open Cabinet critic, John Biffen, the Leader of the House of Commons, was dismissed. Mrs Thatcher later claimed, mordantly: 'he had come to prefer commentary to collective responsibility' [28 p. 589]. Although she lost a 'true believer' in Norman Tebbit, who retired from the Cabinet for a job in the private sector and to spend more time looking after his wife, paralysed in the 1984 Brighton bombing, she felt the moment right to bring back her old favourite, Cecil Parkinson, as Energy Secretary. Mrs Thatcher was also helped by the elevation of several of her earlier opponents such as Pym, St. John Stevas and Prior to the House of Lords where they were limited to 'occasional cautionary noises, of no political significance, from the museum of extinct volcanoes' [76 p. 519]. For those who shared Mrs Thatcher's deep-seated radical drive, all this made for a very promising start.

Further privatisation

As early as July the government's renewed passion for privatisation was demonstrated with the flotation of the British Airports Authority. In December 1988 British Steel also entered the private sector and preparations continued in earnest for the two most controversial sales so far, that of the water and the electricity companies.

Water privatisation had been postponed in July 1986, when the government's authority was at a low ebb and thus ministers had decided not to try to push through a measure that many backbenchers opposed and which was deeply unpopular with the voters. However, despite opinion polls regularly showing that 75 – 80% of the public remained against water privatisation [23 *p. 232*], a bill was reintroduced after the election and the flotation finally occurred in December 1989. The electricity industry was the final privatisation of the Thatcher years. This required a fundamental restructuring of the industry to end the monopoly control enjoyed by the Central Electricity Generating Board (CEGB) over the National Grid, by which electricity was supplied. But it also ran into difficulties over the future of nuclear power. Originally the nuclear industry was to be part of the sell-off, but when the true cost of nuclear power came to light it became clear that its uneconomic costs would prove prohibitive for a private company. Therefore the nuclear power stations remained under government control, but the electricity distribution companies were sold in December 1990 and the privatisation was completed under the Major government with the sale of the generating companies in 1991. The third term thus saw the radicalism of the privatisation pro-gramme continue unabated as the more challenging companies were sold off; but to her critics, now as ever, Mrs Thatcher was 'denationalising out of dogma' [64 *p. 492*].

Education

The third term also saw innovation, which became most evident in social policy, the welfare state being a core ingredient of the Attlean postwar settlement so far largely untouched by her government. Edu-cation was a particular area seen by the Tory right as ripe for reform. A well-aired idea of this school of thought that had found some favour with the leader was the voucher system, a proposal consisting of parents being issued with vouchers which would be exchanged for their children's education. Parents would then shop around, consider-ing schools in both the private and public sector and choose the one they thought best. This would inject the competition, as schools vied for pupils to ensure their survival, which the right-wing believed would improve the quality of education. However, although Mrs Thatcher was attracted to the voucher scheme, she allowed herself to be convinced that political and practical difficulties led to it being a reform too far. But this did not mean there would be no radicalism, as the 1988 Education Reform Act soon proved.

This Act contained two broad reforms. First, a National Curricu-lum of ten foundation subjects, with agreed 'attainment targets' and assessments at the end of the various key stages, at ages seven, eleven, fourteen and sixteen, established to bring consistency nationwide to children's learning. This was clearly a centralising measure as the government took the power to decide what should be in the curriculum. It did not, however, 'allow Ministers simply to write the curriculum' [12 *p. 201*] and working parties of leading experts were established to produce recommendations. Nevertheless, the domination of the centre was demonstrated by Mrs Thatcher's insistence that many aspects of the curriculum should reflect her own personal views. The second thrust of the reform aimed to expand the choice and increase the quality of the schools available. Open enrolment was introduced, which allowed popular schools to expand their intakes. Closely linked to this was the new system of *per capita* funding, which based the level of finance that a school received on the number of pupils on the roll. This produced an incentive to improve standards in order to attract more pupils and therefore more money. Standards were also to be improved by the abolition of the Inner London Education Authority, which to Education Secretary Kenneth Baker: 'had become a byword for swollen bureaucracy, high costs, low academic standards and political extremism' [12 *p. 226*]. Its responsibilities were passed to the individual London Boroughs in the hope that this would save money on unnecessary bureaucracy, which could then be invested in improving the standards of education pupils actually received. Most significantly, the Act gave schools the chance to 'opt-out' of the control of local authorities and receive funding directly from central government. Mrs Thatcher believed that these 'grant maintained (GM) schools' would improve education by allowing 'important decisions to be taken at the level closest to parents and teachers' [28 *p. 592*]. Furthermore, City Technology Colleges (CTCs) were created to teach technical skills, and, together with GM schools, were designed to give parents a greater variety of choice. The drive to introduce greater efficiency and competition extended to higher education. The Act abolished academic tenure, the system by which university academics were appointed for life, as the government believed this provided little incentive to maintain high standards, and the University Grants Commission was replaced by a University Funding Council, to remove the prohibitive cost of expanding the number of students in higher education. These changes had a mixed reception from the education world and were strongly condemned by the universities. There was, however, a general acceptance that their extent was 'revolutionary' [76 *p. 524*], constituting the biggest change to the education system since the 1944 Butler Act.

NHS reform

A second area of social policy that saw radical reform was the National Health Service (NHS). The Griffiths Report of 1983 had already looked at ways of improving the NHS, with the introduction of 200 non-medical managers as a result. Hospitals were also required to put contracts for services such as laundry, cleaning and catering out for 'competitive tendering'. This allowed firms from the public or private sectors to put in an offer to provide the service for a certain price and the firm that offered to provide the service the most efficiently would be awarded the contract. However, for Thatcherites these reforms were only the beginning.

Originally, an overhaul of the NHS had been planned for a Conservative fourth term, but after a crisis in the winter of 1987, when the media was rife with reports of ward closures and cancelled operations, the government decided to act. Therefore, in January 1988, Mrs Thatcher announced that she was to set up a group of ministers to undertake a fundamental review of the NHS. There can be no doubt that the NHS was a very politically sensitive issue, as seen by the uproar following the leak of the 1982 CPRS proposals to end free universal healthcare, and Mrs Thatcher thus accepted that any reforms of the NHS would have to be more limited than some on the free market right of the party were demanding. She therefore ensured that the review group accepted that medical care would be kept 'free at the point of consumption' [28 *p. 609*] realising that to go beyond that would be political suicide.

The results of the review included a decision to promote private health insurance, allowing individuals to offset the cost of premiums against tax liabilities, though Lawson's opposition to this move resulted in tax relief being limited to only those over 60 years of age. The review's decision to focus on structure rather than funding resulted in the key decision to establish the NHS 'internal market'. The White Paper of January 1989 introduced a crucial separation between commissioner and provider to the NHS. Hospitals, the service providers, became self-managing trusts and District Health Authorities (DHA); service commissioners took on the responsibility of identifying the needs of their locality and purchasing the healthcare service required. Although DHAs usually used their local NHS Trust hospital, they also purchased healthcare from other providers in the private sector. Consequently, hospitals in both the private and public sector had to compete for patients and it was planned that this would force the NHS to give value for money and ensure its services were responsive to the needs of patients. Through 'GP fundholding', GPs had the option of controlling their own budgets, an option the government intended that the majority of GPs would take up. With a limited budget (except in cases of clinical need), GPs would have an interest in purchasing services for their patients from only the service providers who offered the best value for money and thus all hospitals would have an incentive to maximise efficiency.

Although these measures were undoubtedly radical and were condemned by the medical professions, appearing to many as 'privatisation run mad' [64 *p. 494*], they left the main principle of the postwar consensus in healthcare, that of *universal* and *free* treatment, unchanged. Although, unlike the education reforms, the NHS reforms were not aimed at reducing the power of local authorities, which it should be remembered had not had control over NHS hospitals since 1948, eroding the power of the so-called 'Looney Left' high-spending local authorities was a theme that ran through many Thatcherite reforms. Nowhere was this more obvious than in Mrs Thatcher's cherished, yet doomed, proposals to replace the domestic rates with the Community Charge.

THE FLAGSHIP HITS THE ROCKS: THE POLL TAX (1985–90)

Right from the beginning of the first term, the Thatcher government had shown itself willing to take on local government. Through the 1980 Housing Act, Environment Secretary Michael Heseltine provided for the sale of council houses on a scale never seen before, allowing them to be sold for a minimum of one-third less than their market value. Some councils initially refused to adopt the policy, but after Heseltine defeated the objections of Norwich Council in the courts other councils were forced to accept the government's demands. Heseltine was also a prime-mover in another crusade, against what Mrs Thatcher had long seen as unjustifiable overspending by some, mostly Labour-controlled, local councils.

Local authority finance came from two main sources: local government grants from central government and the rates, a tax on households based on the notional rental value of their property. Environment Secretary Heseltine had attempted to reduce local authority spending by cutting the central grants of perceived overspenders. However, the response of many Labour-controlled councils was simply to raise their rates to meet any shortfall. This made political sense as the majority of their own supporters were poor enough to qualify for rate rebates, and the increased burden fell on businesses and richer, often Conservative, voters. Solid Labour-controlled authorities could thus increase their revenue with relative political impunity. The government's response was to introduce 'rate capping' in 1984, which allowed the Department of the Environment to reduce rate levels where it considered them excessive. Expenditure was further reduced by simply abolishing heavy-spending councils. The Local Government Act of 1985 put in train the abolition of the Greater London Council (the successor to the London County Council) and six other Metropolitan Authorities, devolving their responsibilities to boroughs and metropolitan districts. Ken Livingstone, the Labour leader of the GLC, put up a strong defence, but could only delay the inevitable. For Mrs Thatcher, however, radical as the above measures were, the problems of local government finance could only be satisfactorily addressed by far-reaching reforms to the whole system of rates.

As far back as 1974, Mrs Thatcher had given an election pledge, as a member of Heath's Shadow Cabinet, to abolish the rates. Although this commitment was a direct concern of Heath's, Mrs Thatcher claims to have personally 'always disliked the rates intensely' [28 *p. 644*] and had criticised them from early in her career. There were popular, long-standing arguments against the rates. It was unfair to have a pensioner paying the same as a neighbouring household containing five or six working adults and as the rates were based on the notional rental value of a home they were seen as an undesirable tax on home improvement.

The possibility of rate reform was first examined in 1981 and the resulting Green Paper produced the familiar alternatives of a local income tax, a sales tax or a poll tax. None seemed desirable. The income tax option was rejected as it was Conservative policy to decrease income tax rather than increasing its burden. The sales tax would have been hopelessly impractical as people would simply travel to find the cheapest authority. And a 'flat rate' (i.e. at the same level for all regardless of means) poll tax was seen as politically unacceptable. However, by the second term there was an added incentive to find a solution. This was because Scottish law obliged the rental values on which the rates in Scotland were based to be revised every five years and the increases that would result from the 1985 revaluation threatened to alienate many Conservative supporters. Furthermore, a revaluation in England and Wales would have a similar effect, and although an English revaluation was not required by law, it could not be postponed indefinitely. Therefore, in September 1984, Mrs Thatcher authorised Environment Secretary Patrick Jenkin to embark on another review of rate reform, the details of which were delegated to his junior ministers William Waldegrave and Kenneth Baker. On 31 March 1985, the review group reported their conclusions to Mrs Thatcher and selected members of the Cabinet at Chequers. It was at this meeting, after a masterful presentation of the group's ideas by Kenneth Baker, that the 'Community Charge was born' [28 *p. 648*]. Against her wishes, the Community Charge rapidly became known publicly as the 'poll tax'.

The tax was to operate on a per capita basis, with local authorities setting the level for their region and receiving all the revenue raised. The Community Charge's chief attraction for Mrs Thatcher was that, as it was a tax on people rather than property, everyone would have to pay (although there were some rebates for the poorest). In contrast, it was estimated that only 12 million out of the 35 million people eligible to vote paid the full rates [28 *p. 645*]. In the past, with many people not affected by rises in the rates, some councils had been able to increase the level with few electoral consequences. With *everyone* paying the Community Charge, effective accountability of local authorities to tax payers would be established. Consequently, electors under high-spending Labour councils would at last feel the pain of extravagant spending, and might then feel inclined to replace the Labour council by a low-spending Conservative one, to gain a lower Community Charge. The Community Charge might thus at the same time reduce public expenditure *and* destroy the powerbase of the Labour Party. However, even at this early stage, the proposal met fierce opposition in the person of Nigel Lawson.

Although Lawson had not been at the Chequers meeting, as soon as he heard about the plans he made his opposition known. Having failed to persuade Mrs Thatcher of the potential problems face to face, he circulated a memorandum which concluded: 'the proposal for a poll tax would be completely unworkable and politically cata-strophic' [23 *p. 574*] [*Doc. 24*]. Lawson argued that it would hit the poor more than the rich, foreshadowing the standard objection of unfairness in that the 'duke paid the same as the dustman'. He also argued that far from increasing accountability, the poll tax would be used as an excuse by local authorities to increase spending and blame the resulting higher charges on central government. Mrs Thatcher and the Cabinet Committee in charge of the poll tax were unconvinced and, with clear support from the Cabinet, the 'flagship' of her third term steamed on.

At this stage it was planned that the tax would be introduced over a ten-year period. Over this period of 'dual running' both the poll tax and the rates would be in operation with the former slowly replacing the latter. However, in May 1986, Nicholas Ridley became Environment Secretary and strongly opposed dual running. He believed that it would be unpopular to have two taxes instead of one and the accountability benefits of the new tax would be obscured. Despite Lawson's opposition, in July 1987 he managed to reduce the dual running period to five years. After the 1987 party conference saw a violent condemnation of even a five-year dual running period, Ridley secured its total abolition. This seemed a triumph of radicalism at the time, with the flagship being so publicly endorsed by the party, but as Mrs Thatcher later admitted: 'it may have been a mistake to do away with ... dual running' [28 p. 654]. The rocks loomed.

Disastrously for the government, the predicted level of the charge, which stood at less than £200 when dual running was abandoned, continued to grow as local authorities increased expenditure in the run-up to the changeover, hard pressed by falling grants from the centre and suspecting that voters would blame central government for the high level of the charge. It soon became clear that most people would be *worse off* as a result of the poll tax (by September 1989 it was estimated that 82% of individuals would pay more than under the rates [28 p. 656]). With the abolition of dual running, this would come as a very sharp shock. The first significant expression of discontent in the Conservative Party came when Michael Mates MP led a rebellion in the House of Commons in April 1988. Mates attempted to amend the legislation so that the tax would be banded into different rates depending on people's ability to pay. The growing unpopularity of the new tax was shown by a reduction in the government's majority from 101 to 25 in defeating the amendment, even after Ridley promised to make the rebates far more generous for the least well off.

Disquiet on the Conservative benches reflected disquiet in the country, which soon turned into open anger when the full extent of the new charges became known. In vain the government sought to decrease the charges and prevent political disaster. In July 1989, grants to local authorities were increased by £2.6 billion, but this proved ineffective as the money was poorly targeted and 'most of the "not-quite-poor" marginal voters were left largely unprotected from the large financial losses to come' [41 p. 140]. The government therefore resorted to capping the highest charges. The decision to cap struck at the idea that councils set their charge and were then accountable to the electorate for it, although Mrs Thatcher had previously trumpeted transparent accountability as one of the tax's greatest merits. In the words of commentator Simon Jenkins: 'capping was a savage blow to the poll tax' [54 pp. 54–5]. When the tax was implemented in

Scotland in April 1989, one year earlier than in England, its massive unpopularity was confirmed: some claimed that up to a half of all Scots withheld at least part of what was due [76 *p. 540*]. But for Mrs Thatcher there could be no question of a U-turn. Not even the electoral disaster of 22 March 1990, when the Conservatives lost the Mid-Staffordshire by-election where they had previously enjoyed a solid majority of 19,000, nor a violent riot in Trafalgar Square on 31 March could persuade her to change course. But for all her gallant resolve, nothing could disguise the fact that, this time, her judgement appeared to be in error.

To her chagrin, Lawson had been proved right: faced with new, drastically higher bills, instead of blaming local authority overspending, the majority of the electorate blamed central government for introducing the tax. Furthermore, instead of reducing public spending, the tax's collection costs, and the increases in central government grant to keep the charge as low as possible are estimated to have actually increased spending by £4 billion [76 *p. 541*] by the time it was abandoned by John Major in 1991. The saga could also be seen as demonstrating the weakness of the British constitution, as commentators have claimed that the government's ability to enact such a disastrous policy highlights the 'absence of checks and balances faced by a government with a secure hold on the Commons' [41 *p. 303*].

However, even years after leaving office, these arguments held little sway with Mrs Thatcher. She had made the poll tax her flagship, and she never lost faith: 'Given time, it would have been seen as one of the most far-reaching and beneficial reforms ever made in the working of local government' [28 *p. 642*] [*Doc. 25*]. But as 1990 drew to a close, this view, like Margaret Thatcher, looked dangerously isolated from reality.

CLASHES WITH COLLEAGUES : DISAGREEMENTS OVER EUROPE AND THE ERM (1987–89)

However, the weakness of Mrs Thatcher's position by 1990 was not solely due to the poll tax. Indeed, from the very beginning of the third term she encountered difficulties as her relationship with her two most senior colleagues, Nigel Lawson and Geoffrey Howe, deteriorated.

Although Mrs Thatcher admits that Lawson occupied a 'leading place' amongst Thatcherite revolutionaries [26 *p. 308*], since 1985 a difference of opinion between the leader and her Chancellor had developed. At its heart lay their views of the European Exchange Rate

Mechanism (ERM), the system by which some European currencies were kept at approximate parities. Britain had not yet joined the system – although the government had been committed to entry when the time was right since June 1979 – and with monetary targets practically abandoned, Lawson argued that membership would provide the discipline necessary to control inflation. Mrs Thatcher disagreed, taking the purer monetarist view that inflation could only be mastered by controlling the money supply. At a meeting of senior ministers in November 1985 the issue of ERM membership first became a matter of open and bitter conflict within the government as Mrs Thatcher found herself heavily outnumbered in opposition to joining. The bad feeling generated by that event was part of the background to the Westland Affair and the issue slowly destroyed her relations with Lawson and Howe.

By 1987, as Lawson's apparent success in managing the economy was playing a key part in Conservative revival, he began to tire of his boss's resistance. In March of that year he began using interest rates and intervention in the currency markets to set the pound's value at DM3.00. However, Mrs Thatcher claimed to have had no knowledge of this change of policy until it was pointed out to her in an interview with the *Financial Times* on 11 November. To Thatcher loyalists such as Nicholas Ridley, Lawson thus joined the ERM 'unilaterally and unofficially' [26 *p. 201*]. Although Lawson disputes Mrs Thatcher's ignorance, it is the undermining of her authority that is surely of greater consequence: a senior minister had caused her government to adopt a new policy of great significance with no prior discussion with the PM or senior colleagues. Futhermore, to Mrs Thatcher, not only was this an unprecedented act of insubordination, but it was likely to reignite inflation and was thus severely misguided.

Lawson brushed her worries aside, claiming he had 'sterilised' the policy through gilt-edged security sales and thus his policy would not fuel inflation. However, after especially heavy intervention by the Bank of England on 2 and 3 March 1988, Mrs Thatcher demanded that Lawson abandon his exchange rate policy and allow the pound to rise above DM3.00. Grudgingly he agreed and on 7 March the pound reached DM3.05. The official Treasury line was that the policy of exchange rate stability remained, but this clashed with Mrs Thatcher's own view that the exchange rate was not a matter for government, but for the markets. This disagreement was about to become public.

On 8 March, Lawson told the Commons that further appreciation of the pound was 'unlikely to be sustainable', but a few minutes later Mrs Thatcher seemed to repudiate attempts to control the exchange rate, claiming that 'there is no way in which one can buck the market' [14 *p. 309*]. It was clear that the Prime Minister and her Chancellor were not at one over exchange rate policy and by Sunday 13 March reports of a rift appeared in the press [*Doc. 26*]. Mrs Thatcher considered sacking Lawson, but after his high-profile 1988 Budget this was out of the question. The Budget, on 15 March, reduced the basic rate of tax from 27p to 25p and the higher rate from 60p to 40p and was widely seen as a triumph by the party. For the time being he was safe. Furthermore, on 16 May, after an 'immensely damaging performance' [23 *p. 834*] in the Commons four days earlier when Mrs Thatcher refused to say she agreed with her Chancellor over exchange rate policy, she finally agreed to endorse his stance [*Doc. 27*]. While this may have ended the public row, their private relationship continued to deteriorate.

As 1988 wore on, the economic climate worsened, and by July the current account payments deficit stood at a massive £20 billion. Worse, inflation began to rise again, and Lawson was forced to raise interest rates rapidly from their low of 7.5% in May to 12% in August. Mrs Thatcher, clinging to monetarist principles, believed that Lawson's Deutschmark shadowing had led to monetary policy being too loose, thus allowing inflation to rise. Therefore by this stage she was 'in a permanent state of resentment' with her Chancellor [23 *p. 850*] as she blamed him for throwing away the government's hard-won economic success.

Any resentment she was feeling towards Lawson was matched, if not excelled, by her feelings towards her other principal lieutenant, Geoffrey Howe. Howe was another founder member of Mrs Thatcher's premiership and although they had been close early on, since the 1987 election their personal relationship had rapidly deteriorated. As Mrs Thatcher became increasingly sceptical over Europe after the 1986 Single European Act, Howe adopted a more pro-European stance which Mrs Thatcher saw as 'misty Europeanism ... an almost romantic longing for Britain to become part of some grandiose consensus' [28 *p. 309*]. Furthermore, Howe had infuriated her by openly siding with Lawson during the exchange rate row, and by questioning the ERM 'time is right' formula at a speech in Perth on 13 May, saying: 'we cannot go on forever adding that qualification to the underlying commitment' [21 *p. 575*]. Mrs Thatcher's dislike of European centralism was, for her, another objection to the ERM and she chose to set out her fears in a speech in Bruges on 20 September 1988.

Despite the efforts of the Foreign Office to temper the leader's hostility, the speech was seen as a 'watershed' [76 *p. 550*]. It was a clear exposition of Mrs Thatcher's opposition to the way many Europeans, notably the Commission President Jacques Delors, hoped that the EC would develop. She proclaimed: 'We have not successfully rolled back the frontiers of the state in Britain only to see them reimposed at a European level'. She also called for co-operation between 'independent sovereign states' rather than integration which she lambasted as trying to create 'some sort of identikit Euro-personality' [30 p. 319] [Doc. 28]. Howe was 'deeply dismayed by the Bruges speech' [21 p. 538]. While he firmly opposed a federal European superstate, he believed that Europe would only be made stronger with 'the sacrifice of political independence and the rights of national parliaments' [21 p. 536]. As well as seeking to tap into populist distrust of the EC, Mrs Thatcher used the Bruges speech to put Howe, and other pro-Europeans in the party, in their place by demonstrating her continued hostility to European integration and therefore by implication, membership of the ERM.

Her opponents, however, refused to accept defeat. The whole European debate erupted again with the publication of the Delors Report in April 1989, which planned for European Economic and Monetary Union (EMU) to be achieved in three stages: it suggested that if a country accepted the first stage (ERM membership), it would be bound to continue with the remaining two stages. This was unacceptable to Mrs Thatcher, as well as to Lawson and Howe. But Lawson and Howe were divided from Mrs Thatcher by their belief that it was desirable for Britain to take part in stage one (i.e. ERM membership), providing that this did not automatically require participation in the further two stages which would require unification of currencies and the end of sterling's independence. If Britain was able to demonstrate goodwill by joining the ERM, then Howe and Lawson believed that the government would be in a much stronger position to influence developments in the EC about which it had severe reservations, such as full EMU.

Mrs Thatcher's hostile tone towards the EC in the run up to the European elections of June 1989, in which the Conservatives lost a humiliating 13 of their 45 seats, was far from what Howe and Lawson were hoping for. Therefore, with the Delors Report due to be discussed at the Madrid EC Summit at the end of June, Howe and Lawson, acting increasingly as co-partners, decided to set out their views beforehand on the best way of proceeding. A joint minute of 14 June thus proposed that to avoid isolation at Madrid, which could permanently harm Britain's interests, Mrs Thatcher should be prepared to give a non-legally binding commitment to join the ERM by the end of 1992. This would be subject to agreement that the pound's ERM level would have wide margins, and all countries had abolished exchange controls. The minute concluded by requesting a joint meeting with Mrs Thatcher to discuss the issues.

It could be seen as only natural for the Chancellor and Foreign Secretary to wish to discuss the government's response to these issues, as the decisions to be taken at Madrid would have far-reaching consequences for Britain's future. However, Mrs Thatcher saw the minute as an 'ambush' and was reluctant to agree to a meeting. After she did agree to see Howe and Lawson, on 20 June, she told them that she thought their analysis entirely mistaken and the meeting ended with no agreement. The next day, Howe received a minute from her office that contained an 'alternative way of proceeding'. This added a series of demanding economic conditions that would have to be met before Britain would join the ERM – that is, it was an attempt to delay joining for as long as possible. This was far from the positive response that Howe and Lawson saw as essential. They therefore sent another minute restating their original points and requesting a further meeting. Mrs Thatcher again tried very hard to avoid this meeting, but eventually agreed to see the pair on 25 June. The atmosphere was tense. Howe restated his case and said that if Mrs Thatcher refused his advice he would be forced to resign. Lawson twisted the knife: 'You should know Prime Minister, that if Geoffrey goes, I must go too' [23 *p. 933*].

Mrs Thatcher said nothing, although she was livid, and later that day she set off for Madrid with her Foreign Secretary. She refused to speak to him before the Summit and the ground was wide open as she took her place at the summit table. In the end, as she conceded no precise *date* for ERM entry, and there were no resignations, she claimed to have called her colleagues' bluff successfully. However, for Howe and Lawson, the date of entry was just a detail. What they had wanted was a more positive attitude towards Europe, and Mrs Thatcher seemed to have provided this, sticking far more closely to their suggested negotiating position than the 'alternative way of proceeding'. Lawson believes that the Madrid developments were 'universally interpreted ... as a major new development and a big step towards ERM membership' [23 *p. 924*]. Mrs Thatcher had lost the battle, but not yet the war [*Docs 29, 30 and 31*].

With her authority badly damaged, Mrs Thatcher was swift to act. On 24 July Howe was summoned to Downing Street to be told, to his absolute amazement, that he was being removed from the Foreign Office. Mrs Thatcher offered him the job of Leader of the House of

Commons or Home Secretary, together with the official residence of Dorneywood, currently occupied by the unsuspecting Lawson. After a day in which a devastated Howe contemplated resignation, he finally accepted Leader of the House of Commons provided that he also assumed the title of Deputy Prime Minister. But as he had demanded the title, his post was little more than titular: Howe was never to occupy the special position held by Willie Whitelaw until his resignation in January 1988 after a stroke [*Doc. 32*]. Howe's place as Foreign Secretary was taken by an unsuspecting John Major, who had only held the junior Cabinet post of Chief Secretary and was the most inexperienced Conservative Foreign Secretary since Selwyn Lloyd in 1955. However, one unfortunate effect of the reshuffle was to infuriate Douglas Hurd, the Home Secretary, as it emerged that Mrs Thatcher had offered his job to Howe without even consulting him. Hurd was insulted, Howe was seething, but it was Lawson who was about to rock the boat.

It should by now be clear that the third term was, on the whole, not a happy time for Nigel Lawson. However, the fateful month must have been May 1989 when Sir Alan Walters resumed his post as economic advisor to the Prime Minister. Walters had held this post from 1981 to 1984 and now returned as pure a monetarist as ever, opposed to fixed exchange rates in principle and believing that the ERM was 'the work of the devil' [*14 p. 311*]. Lawson was deeply concerned, and had tried to block Walters' appointment, claiming that it could exacerbate divisions in the government. Nevertheless, Mrs Thatcher was determined that Walters should return, as an alternative source of economic advice to Lawson and the Treasury, and therefore dismissed his concerns.

Lawson's fears seemed to have been justified when soon after Walters' return, stories of his opposition to Lawson's policies began to appear in the press [*Doc. 33*]. These culminated in the appearance, in the *Financial Times* on 18 October 1989, of extracts from an article that Walters had written. Although he had written it before returning to Number Ten, he now chose to publish it, and it stressed that he was continuing to advise Mrs Thatcher strongly against joining the ERM. Lawson felt that his position was being made untenable as his authority over economic policy was being undermined by proclamations from an advisor who was known to be very influential with the Prime Minister: 'The markets heard two voices and did not know which to believe' [*23 p. 961*].

Therefore, on 26 October Lawson told Mrs Thatcher that his position had become impossible and that if she did not dismiss Walters by the end of the year, he himself would have to resign. Mrs Thatcher was genuinely surprised by what she heard and at several meetings throughout the day tried to persuade him to stay. However, the one concession that may have persuaded him was withheld. Walters was on no account to go. Therefore, at 6 pm, it was announced that Nigel Lawson had resigned [*Doc. 34*]. The government was shaken to its very foundations, as is to be expected when a Chancellor of the Exchequer, and one of six years standing, resigns after a policy dispute with the Prime Minister. Two days later Mrs Thatcher told the interviewer Brian Walden that she believed Lawson's position as Chancellor had been 'unassailable' [76 *p. 563*]: it would not be long before others in the party would begin to question whether her own position was similarly 'unassailable'.

AFTER NIGEL: THE PRIME MINISTER LOSES HER WAY (1989–90)

In the immediate aftermath of Lawson's resignation, Walters insisted on resigning himself and John Major, after only 94 days as Foreign Secretary, was appointed Chancellor. Although Lawson's detractors claimed that Walters was just a pretext and the true reasons behind his resignation lay elsewhere ('Lawson knew the economy was going badly wrong and he knew he was entirely and solely responsible' [26 *p. 216*]), others were less convinced and there can be no doubt that his resignation gravely weakened Mrs Thatcher's authority. By late 1989, the impression of a government in disarray was confounded by severe worries over the unpopularity of the poll tax and the apparent poor state of the economy, breeding open discontent on the backbenches.

Disquiet with Mrs Thatcher's 'autocratic' style of leadership, an alleged loss of consultation and perhaps judgement after Whitelaw's departure, and concern at an over-reliance on courtiers in Number Ten, notably Press Secretary Bernard Ingham and Private Secretary Charles Powell, at the expense of elected politicians, all contributed to the discontent. She was felt to be an increasingly isolated premier, far removed from the lady who promised a more consultative style of leadership when she ousted Heath in 1975. Unrest surfaced when Anthony Meyer challenged Mrs Thatcher for the leadership of the party in November 1989, an eventuality no one in their right mind would have predicted just 18 months before. Although party rules required Mrs Thatcher to submit herself for re-election every year, this had become a formality as, for the 14 years since Heath's departure, no one had put themselves forward as an alternative. There was even speculation that she would be challenged that November by a political heavyweight, rather than by a non-serious candidate who put himself forward merely to test the water, and even Geoffrey Howe admits to having pondered his chances [21 *pp. 609–10*]. The results of the vote on 5 December were: Thatcher, 314; Meyer, 33. Mrs Thatcher thus managed to fend off any immediate threat to her leadership and she saw the outcome as 'by no means unsatisfactory' [28 *p. 830*]. The crude results, however, were misleading. Although only 33 MPs had voted against Mrs Thatcher, another 27 had withheld support by abstaining or spoiling their papers. Furthermore, many had made it clear to her campaign manager, George Younger, that their support was given on a probationary basis only. With hindsight, Denis Thatcher's verdict, that 'we had too many people voting against her' [74 *p. 256*], proved more accurate than his wife's assessment.

Mrs Thatcher badly needed a period of stability and political success to recover her authority and composure. By April 1990 opinion polls gave Labour a lead over the Conservatives that averaged at 22% [76 *p. 569*]. For Tory optimists, the May local elections provided a glimmer of hope as despite predictions of a 600-seat net loss, the Conservatives managed to lose only 172 in net terms. Labour's lead had dropped to 8% by September [12 *p. 348*], and while the recession gripped tighter, Party Chairman Ken Baker's 'Summer Heat on Labour', with its direct attacks on Neil Kinnock, imparted an air of optimism to the Tories. Mrs Thatcher's outright hostility to the ERM, which had caused so many problems during the third term, also showed some signs of being contained. This was shown by Major's success in persuading her to allow Britain to take a positive initiative towards Europe by the 'hard ECU' proposal announced on 20 June. This suggested that a real parallel European currency be established that *could* develop into a single currency in the future. Although Mrs Thatcher undermined Major's attempts to sell this idea to the European leaders by stressing her continued opposition to a single currency [8 *24.6.90*], and the proposal found little real support in Europe, it was a step forward. More significantly, however, was Mrs Thatcher's private concession to Major, of 13 June, that she would 'not resist sterling joining the ERM' [28 *p. 722*]. Sterling duly joined on 8 October, but Mrs Thatcher received little credit. Her opposition had been well known and agreeing to join was seen not as pragmatism and a new spirit of moderation but as a sign of weakness as she could no longer carry the Cabinet on this issue.

Mrs Thatcher's isolation within the Cabinet was made almost complete on 14 July when Nicholas Ridley tendered his resignation.

Ridley had given an interview to Dominic Lawson, Nigel's son, editor of *The Spectator,* in which he had expressed views on Europe that caused much offence. He called EMU: 'a German racket designed to take over the whole of Europe' and implied similarities between Europe's present leaders and Adolf Hitler [*Doc. 35*]. Ridley was the last unquestionably loyal Thatcherite ideologue and she fought hard to keep him, but with the media 'wild with righteous indignation' [26 *p.* 224], he had little choice but to resign. Not only did this leave Mrs Thatcher isolated in the Cabinet, but it compounded the charge that her government was falling apart as two other ministers, Norman Fowler (in January) and Peter Walker (in June), had abandoned ship earlier in the year. Another problem was thus added to the bloated catalogue of predicaments which the Thatcher government now faced. But if the domestic scene looked dire, perhaps the key to a revival in Mrs Thatcher's fortune lay in the Middle East.

On 2 August Iraq invaded Kuwait. This unprovoked aggression by the Iraqi leader, Saddam Hussein, received world-wide condemnation and, by chance, Mrs Thatcher was visiting the American President, George Bush, in Colorado at the time of the invasion. Relations with America had cooled markedly since Bush assumed the Presidency in 1989, as he wanted to distance himself from Reagan who had been criticised for allowing Mrs Thatcher too much influence. Bush had even referred to a 'partnership in leadership' between the United States and Germany, rather than Britain, in Mainz on 31 May. However, the Gulf crisis allowed the 'special relationship' between Britain and America to flower once again, as Mrs Thatcher joined Bush in condemning the aggression. She also provided him with steadfast support throughout the crisis. When it appeared that economic sanctions would have little effect on Hussein's resolve, Mrs Thatcher lived up to her strong rhetoric by sending the 7th Armoured Brigade to make up part of the multi-national force that was eventually to liberate Kuwait.

However, any Thatcherites harbouring hopes that Saddam Hussein would provide a distraction similar to Galtieri in 1982 were to be bitterly disappointed. It was clear that the Falklands affair, where British sovereignty had been violated, was very different from the American-led expedition to free the oil-rich Kuwait. Although Mrs Thatcher may have gained some public support from her strong line against the Iraqi aggression, to the British electorate Iraq was little more than a 'side-show' [76 *p. 574*]. As the Autumn of 1990 drew in, attention remained firmly focused on the home front, where a drama of epic proportions was about to unfold.

5 THE END OF AN ERA

JITTERY OCTOBER (1990)

Mrs Thatcher remained deeply unhappy about Britain's entry into the ERM on 8 October, but as her close aide Charles Powell later admitted: 'The truth is that she was in a tiny minority in the government always in opposing joining the ERM and she fought off attempt after attempt to do it' [70 p. 111]. Mrs Thatcher was deeply angry: she realised she had been outmanoeuvred over entry, and became even more implacably opposed to any further manifestation of European centralisation.

At the annual party conference, held that year in Bournemouth, she was testy and not on her best form. Her speech on 12 October saw an ill-advised reference to the Liberal Democrats as a 'dead parrot', while her words of support for ERM entry – scrutinised with surgical precision – were noticeably tepid. Her fury was saved, however, for the Delors project and full monetary union: EMU, she said, 'would be entering a federal Europe through the back-Delors'.

On 18 October, the second terrible by-election of the year for the Tories took place (the first had been at Mid-Staffordshire in March). Occasioned by the IRA's murder of Eastbourne's Tory MP, her former PPS Ian Gow, the party lost the seat to the Liberal Democrats, the 'dead parrot' of just six days earlier, with a swing of 20 per cent. The mild mood of optimism among the Tories over the summer rapidly evaporated, and at the worst possible time for Mrs Thatcher, with the opportunity still alive for her to be challenged for the leadership that November.

A European Council meeting in Rome rekindled the embers of division in the party over Europe, subdued since ERM entry, soon producing a roaring blaze. Questioned on 28 October in the House of Commons on her return from Rome, Mrs Thatcher uttered three of her most memorable words, 'No! No! No!' to indicate her views on Delors' vision for the future of Europe. Sitting next to her on the front bench was her Deputy Prime Minister and erstwhile friend, Geoffrey Howe. To him, her antagonism towards the European Community had gone beyond the pale. On 1 November, he announced he would, like Lawson before him, be resigning from her government. Howe may not have been a charismatic figure, or one with a large personal following, but he had been a principal architect of Thatcherism, a former Chancellor of the Exchequer and Foreign Secretary. Coming only one year after Lawson's resignation, Howe's departure made even loyal Tory MPs feel that perhaps she now had to go.

A CHALLENGE EMERGES (EARLY NOVEMBER 1990)

Mrs Thatcher was by now desperately isolated. With Nicholas Ridley's departure from the government that summer, she had lost her last personal friend in the Cabinet. The economy was moving further into recession, her flagship policy of the poll tax was in deep trouble and she was outnumbered by critics, indeed almost friendless, in Cabinet, reminiscent of her earliest days as leader. Following the Eastbourne by-election defeat, Tory MPs began to ask whether they themselves would be able to hang on to their parliamentary seats in the next general election (at most 18 months away) as long as she remained in Downing Street.

Michael Heseltine had been licking his wounds since he walked out of the Cabinet, and her government, over the Westland affair in January 1986. A man with a big ambition to be leader, with a clear set of policies different from Mrs Thatcher's, and with a large personal following, he sensed his moment of history had arrived. He tested the water in a letter to his constituency association chairman on 3 November, widely reported in the Sunday papers the next day. A strong counter-attack against the Heseltine gambit was smartly launched by Party Chairman, Ken Baker, and by Number Ten. Polls on the relative merits of Thatcher and Heseltine – this time around no one was talking about a 'stalking horse': Heseltine was the real thing – were conducted across the media. Frenetic behind-the-scenes lobbying and arm-twisting took place, with Mrs Thatcher coming out on top at this early stage. While Cranley Onslow, chairman of the Tories' 1922 Committee, advanced the date to 15 November for notification to him by any challenger as a way of deterring any possible candidates, Heseltine's constituency chairman responded to his MP on 7 November with a Thatcher loyalist letter, discouraging him from throwing down the gauntlet. Heseltine backed off, declaring that Mrs Thatcher would lead the party into the next general election. It seemed that Mrs Thatcher had survived for another year. Further-more, although initial gains for Mrs Thatcher's popularity as a result of her reaction to the August invasion of Kuwait were limited, as a war seemed ever more likely, it appeared that this foreign adventure might yet show the nation her mettle and restore confidence in her leadership. Perhaps when actual hostilities began, a 'Kuwait factor' similar to the boost she received from the 'Falklands factor' in 1982 might finally appear.

She had not reckoned on Geoffrey Howe. For the few days that followed his resignation on 1 November he bided his time and held his own counsel. He noted the crushing defeats for the party in the by-elections on 8 November in Bradford North and Bootle, and the wide unease with her leadership of the party. Rejecting the idea of standing for leader against her himself, he chose instead to make a major pronouncement on the reasons behind his resignation. This he made in a Commons speech, two days before the closing date for nominations for a leadership challenge.

Mrs Thatcher never forgave Howe for his speech, which she and her followers regarded as an act of disloyalty from a man whose polit-ical career, they felt, she had made. But to Howe, her increasingly hostile stance on Europe had placed an impossible conflict of loyalty on him: to her, and to the national interest. He chose the latter, believing as a former Foreign Secretary of six years' standing that he could not see Britain's interests abroad suffer still further at the hands of what he saw as an isolated and out-of-touch premier. He told a hushed House of Commons that he could no longer serve such a leader, while it was up to others to consider their 'own response' to the crisis [*Doc. 36*]. The speech was seen as an invitation for others to come forward and challenge her, and one contemporary observer described the immediate impact thus: 'Many Conservative MPs last night believed that they had witnessed the undoing of the Prime Min-ister' [2 *14.11.90*]. To Mrs Thatcher, Howe's speech was a 'final act of bile and treachery', and that 'the character he assassinated was in the end his own' [28 *p. 840*].

Howe's speech, and the reaction to it, emboldened Heseltine to pick up his cudgels again, even if he lacked his constituency associa-tion's support. The next day, 14 November, the day before nomina-tions for the election closed, saw Heseltine formally announce his candidature. Mrs Thatcher was furious, but quietly confident, believ-ing Heseltine had too many enemies, both personal and political, to unseat her. The first ballot was to be on 20 November, leaving but a brief time for campaigning. Mrs Thatcher asked Hurd, her Foreign

Secretary, to nominate her, and Major, her Chancellor, to second her, while asking her Parliamentary Private Secretary, Peter Morrison, to organise her campaign. No Airey Neave (her 1975 campaign manager) and in Alan Clark MP's view 'useless' [13 *p. 355*], Morrison was to be widely if unfairly blamed for organising a lacklustre campaign. Neither Hurd (a wholehearted pro-European) nor Major (middle-of-the-road on Europe) were particularly keen to support her on that first ballot. But both were men of ingrained loyalty, and responded to their duty. Both had leadership ambitions of their own. Major, later to be blamed by the Thatcherites for being insufficiently robust in her defence, confided to an aide on 16 November, the day he went into hospital for a wisdom tooth operation, that he thought she was 'finished' [70 *p. 121*], while Hurd intimated on 17 November that he would be willing to stand in a second ballot.

On Sunday 18 November, Mrs Thatcher flew to Paris for a security conference, assured by her aides that she need not worry about being absent, and that she would come safely home in Tuesday's first ballot. She was not encouraged, however, by the Sunday newspapers, many of which said Heseltine deserved to win. Reform of the poll tax was the main issue that divided them, with Europe a second theme. But the real issue was about leadership style, and who would be the more likely to win the 1991 or 1992 general election for the Tories.

Leaving London in fact proved a serious error for Mrs Thatcher. Political parlours were abuzz on the Sunday and Monday as the conventional wisdom took root that she would not beat Heseltine in the first ballot sufficiently decisively for her to be able to carry on. It was assumed that she would then stand down, in which case the lens of the political world would become fixed on the three leading successors, Heseltine, Hurd and Major. Mrs Thatcher was right about one thing: there *was* a big anti–Heseltine feeling among Tory MPs, and once they had been convinced, or convinced themselves, that she would not win, the hunt was on to find the best 'stop Heseltine' candidate. That boiled down to Hurd and Major. Both had their backers. The Old Etonian Hurd appealed more to the establishment and traditionalist wing of the party: the non-public school and apparently Thatcherite Major attracted the support of those who, in figures like Mrs Thatcher and Norman Tebbit, had found an attractive new style of meritocratic and patriotic free-enterprise Toryism.

Polling day, Tuesday 20 November, arrived with Mrs Thatcher still in Paris. The ballot, in common with Tory tradition, was conducted by the 1922 Committee, and at 6.30 pm its chairman, Cranley Onslow, declared that Mrs Thatcher had won 204 votes, and Heseltine 152. A victory for Mrs Thatcher? Well, no, because her margin of victory was four votes short of the number required by the complex 1922 Committee's rules to avoid a second ballot (formally, just two MPs voting for her rather than for Heseltine would have put her in the clear, although it is likely that in reality such a narrow victory would have fatally damaged her authority).

But Mrs Thatcher, true to her character, was not prepared to stand down. Hurd, who was with her in Paris, ever loyal, said that he would support her in the second ballot, promising both his and Major's support. Fortified by this news, she met the press and declared that while she was naturally disappointed to have fallen short of the required first-round votes necessary for outright victory, she would go forward and win the second round. Hurd followed her and lamented the party's in-fighting, publicly pledging his full support to her cause. Confident her words would reverberate around political London, the arch anti-federalist went off with President Mitterrand of France to Versailles for the evening.

THE LADY BOWS OUT (LATE NOVEMBER 1990)

Her resolute declaration to continue in the fray caused widespread dismay in Conservative circles back in Britain. Few had anticipated her staying in the ring. Her doing so, thereby freezing out Major and Hurd, opened up the grave possibility of a victory by anti-free market, pro-Europe Heseltine, who was distrusted by many loyalists since his theatrical departure from the Cabinet, and before. By the time Mrs Thatcher returned to London on Wednesday 21 November, very few Thatcher die-hards – not even husband Denis – believed she should stay on. Like a fading Hollywood star, she toured the corridors of Parliament trying to drum up support from listless MPs, and she appointed the energetic and respected John Wakeham as her new campaign manager.

She had convinced herself she could win in the second ballot, and was therefore mortified when that Wednesday evening she saw a succession of senior Tories, including most of her Cabinet, all of whom (with the odd exception) told her that in their opinion she could not win, although they personally would support her. She regarded their protestations of loyalty as 'weasel words whereby they transmuted their betrayal into frank advice and concern for my fate' [28 *p. 850*]. Wakeham even told her he was encountering problems putting together a campaign team for her. Whether pre-orchestrated or not, the truth was that the Tory establishment had convinced itself that she had to go. She realised that too overnight, and at 7.30 am on Thursday morning she telephoned her most senior official to say that she was going to resign, and plans would have to be made for her to visit the Queen to tell her.

Who did she want to succeed her? Mrs Thatcher had had a stream of men she was at one time grooming as her possible successor. Cecil Parkinson's prospects floundered after news broke of his affair with his secretary, Sara Keays. John Moore, another self-made man of the right, fell from grace when his health crumbled in 1988. That left John Major in the frame, fortunate that his meteoric rise peaked at the moment Mrs Thatcher was disintegrating, and before she discovered that he was not a 'true believer' in the Thatcherite cause. At Cabinet on the morning of Thursday 22 November she tearfully told a silent body of her decision to resign, urging ministers to unite behind the figure most likely to defeat Heseltine. As expected, it was to be a three-horse race.

Mrs Thatcher remained Prime Minister for a further week. During that time, she worked tirelessly to advance Major's interests, phoning newspaper editors and friends and telling them that they had to back him if her revolution was to be secure. Despite Major openly declaring on television 'I am not running as son of Margaret Thatcher. I am running as myself with my own priorities and my own programme', the fact remained that he was seen by Tory MPs as the most Thatcherite of the three contenders. On 27 November, the vote was held: Hurd, 57; Heseltine, 131; Major, 185. Heseltine and Hurd graciously conceded, leaving the space free for Major. Aged just 47, he became the youngest Prime Minister of the century (until Tony Blair in 1997).

At 9.45 am on 28 November 1990, a tearful Mrs Thatcher was driven to Buckingham Palace to tender her resignation as Prime Minister. Her eleven-and-a-half year spell, which began on 4 May 1979, had drawn to a close.

PART THREE: ASSESSMENT

6 BRITAIN UNDER THATCHER

Did Mrs Thatcher's government change Britain? If so, in what ways was the country, and its position in the world, different in November 1990 from where it had been in May 1979? These are deceptively simple questions which do not yield straightforward answers. One can never know how much change would have occurred if another political party or a different Conservative premier had been in power. For a history series it is also particularly appropriate to note that the Thatcher government's impact will look very different in the year 2000 compared to the way it will appear 30, or even 100, years after her fall from power. Consider how an evaluation of Elizabeth I's reign might differ whether the judgement were made in the year of her death, 1603, in 1613, 1633 or even 1703. Historical judgement is dynamic: but, with good quality evidence and a critical intellect, important judgements could have been made about Elizabeth I in 1613. That is the position we are now at.

MACROECONOMICS

Macroeconomic policy changed significantly under Mrs Thatcher. Under her premiership, the monetarist policies pursued by the Callaghan government were intensified. From 1976, Denis Healey, the Labour Chancellor, and Treasury officials began to realise the importance of control of the money supply and credit as a tool of macroeconomic management, a shift in policy rendered unavoidable by the government's reliance on IMF credit after November 1976. To Mrs Thatcher, and her first Chancellor Geoffrey Howe, it was the *only* important macroeconomic tool that the government should be using. Thus incomes policy and price controls were abandoned by the incoming government in 1979.

But the function of macroeconomic policy also changed, with enduring effect. The Thatcher governments abandoned the idea –

dominant for much of the postwar period – that the enlightened management of macroeconomic policy could ensure prosperity; the Keynesian approach to macroeconomic policy was overthrown. The role of macroeconomic policy was reduced to controlling inflation, and the use of fiscal policy to even out the effects of the economic cycle was replaced by an aspiration to balanced budgets – 'good housekeeping'. Long-term economic strength would be achieved not simply by low inflation but also by microeconomic ('supply-side') measures to make the economy operate more efficiently, such as tax reform, privatisation and restriction of trade union power.

Control of the money supply, as codified in the MTFS, became the basis for macroeconomic policy in the early years of the new government. The MTFS outlined targets for public spending, public borrowing and money supply over a four-year period, and the government pledged its political credit to the achievement of these targets in the hope of driving out inflationary expectations rooted in much of the economy after the experience of high inflation in the 1970s. The shock administered by the 1981 Budget had a similar purpose.

But while inflation fell dramatically in the early 1980s, control of the money supply proved a fallible approach. Most of the MTFS's monetary targets were missed and the measurement of the money supply proved an object of intractable dispute. Even Mrs Thatcher herself came to accept the recession of 1980/81 had been aggravated by too tight a monetary policy. Financial deregulation made the situation worse. Under Nigel Lawson as Chancellor the search began for a reformulated monetarism, and by 1985 many in the government were convinced that targeting the exchange rate would achieve the goals which control of the money supply had originally been expected to deliver. This was a view Mrs Thatcher never accepted, with divisive and ultimately fatal consequences for her premiership.

What of the success of the policy? Inflation was cut from 18% in 1980 to 3% in 1986. But in the month of her fall, November 1990, it had risen to 9.7%, a month past its 10.9% peak. The economy was in recession, with output falling at annual rates of 3.5, 2.8, 4.0 and 2.0% in the last two quarters of 1990 and the first two quarters of 1991. Only in one year, 1984, was Britain's inflation rate lower than the average among its G7 competitor nations. Unemployment, which had risen steadily from 1979 to 1986 to over 3 million, fell over 44 consecutive months until early 1990. But then it rose again, from 1.6 million to 1.8 million by late 1990 [58 *p. 173*]. Manufacturing employment dropped by more than 2 million in the 1980s. One can now see that errors were made in 1979–81, in persisting with restrictive policies that did lasting damage to Britain's manufacturing sector. Furthermore, the loose economic stance of 1987–88 allowed inflation to rise again. Christopher Johnson concludes his survey of Mrs Thatcher's economic policy thus: 'the government threw away its achievements by allowing demand to expand too quickly, letting inflation rise again to the double-figure level it had inherited ... the battle against inflation was a Phyrrhic victory, at an unacceptable cost in unemployment' [*55 p. 258*].

Another central goal of macroeconomic policy was controlling the growth in public expenditure. Public spending fell from 44% of GDP in 1979 to just under 40% by 1990, a considerable achievement when it is remembered that expenditure rose significantly in many other European countries over this period. Through controlling public expenditure, the government was able to use the fiscal dividend from increased growth to lower direct taxes and thus cultivate the Conservative electoral base. The Thatcher legacy on public expenditure was to diminish the allure of big government and led to election promises from both main parties centring more on low taxes and less on big-spending.

THE SUPPLY SIDE

Privatisation was the most conspicuously successful supply-side aspect, albeit not one which was a top priority when Mrs Thatcher came to power in 1979. Early successes with privatising state industries turned an *ad hoc* initiative into a core policy plank of her administration. She came to see herself having a mission to reverse the Attlee government's great swathe of nationalisations of 1945–51, vital not just to reducing the size of the state sector and increasing the size of the more efficient private sector, but also as a means of spreading share ownership, which was part of her 'popular capitalism' vision. According to one seasoned commentator: 'privatisation was probably the most far-reaching achievement of the Thatcher era' [*67 p. 229*].

The turning point was the £3,900 million sale of (half of) British Telecom in 1984. The high popular demand for shares, the windfall profit to the government and the philosophical neatness of transferring state assets to private hands are all facets she found vastly attractive. Objections to expanding privatisation from Whitehall (which, led by the Treasury, later became an enthusiast for privatisation) and legal difficulties were all swept aside. So too were concerns that some of the big sell-offs, such as British Gas and British Telecom, were merely transferring public monopolies to private hands, and not engendering real competition. When the government bowed to pressure and introduced some competition, it was in a highly qualified and regulated form. By November 1990, 50 big companies had been sold off or were earmarked for sale, which included over two-thirds of the industrial assets owned by the state in 1979. The number of private shareholders rose from 3 million in 1979 to 9 million in 1990 (a figure that subsequently fell). After 1990, John Major was left with either the more difficult, or the more marginal, state assets to privatise. The privatisation policy marked a sea-change in postwar British history: the government of Tony Blair resisted 'renationalising' privatised industries and services, and instead looked for its own ways of bringing market disciplines to bear on the state sector.

The same anti-statist, 'self-help' philosophy could be found in the policy of refusing to prop up crumbling companies (in contrast to the policies of the immediate Labour and Conservative government predecessors) and in cutting industrial and regional subsidies. Inner-city renewal countenanced government aid, helping small businesses to establish themselves, but then the state withdrew its support and the new enterprises had to swim alone, or sink. To free up enterprise, business and personal taxation were radically recast: an early measure cut the top rate of tax on earned income from 83 to 60 and later to 40 pence in the pound. Capital gains tax was reduced, as was tax on small companies. Critics pointed out that whereas the *direct* tax burden certainly fell, indirect tax (such as VAT) and other tax increases meant that the aggregate tax burden rose during the Thatcher years. Further supply-side reforms were the deregulation of the banks, building societies and the City. The abolition of exchange controls in 1979, which at last made sterling freely convertible, was arguably the most important liberalisation, easing the way for UK companies to build up assets abroad, a move mirrored by a sharp increase in foreign investment over the 1980s. It was a formidable array of philosophically-linked measures, which were accepted and even added to by successor Tory and Labour administrations.

TRADE UNION REFORM

A final supply-side reform was to the labour market. Influenced by thinkers like F. A. Hayek, Mrs Thatcher was concerned to bolster the operation of the market economy by freeing up the supply of labour: if that meant restricting the collective rights of workers in trade unions, so be it. A reduction in the political power of trade unions was a clear Thatcherite objective. She was aided by union unpopularity, heightened above all by their role in the 'winter of discontent' (1978–79), and by widespread beliefs, encouraged by an unsympathetic press, that trade unions had become overpowerful and insufficiently accountable.

Rather than opting for a blunderbuss piece of legislation, as had been tried by her predecessor as Conservative leader, Heath, in the form of the 1971 Industrial Relations Act, Mrs Thatcher chose incrementalism. The 1980 (Prior) Employment Act outlawed secondary picketing and restricted the operation of the 'closed shop'. The 1982 (Tebbit) Employment Act made unions liable for damages if held responsible for unlawful industrial action, while narrowing the definition of a 'lawful' trade dispute, and strengthening individuals' protection against closed shops. The 1984 (King) Trade Union Act required secret ballots and made unions liable for damages incurred during a strike unless a majority for strike action had been secured by prior secret ballot, while the 1988 (Fowler) Employment Act gave members still further powers *vis-à-vis* their trade unions. In sum, the measures brought the unions back within the scope of civil law, greatly narrowing the blanket immunity from civil action they had acquired in the 1906 Trade Disputes Act. Political strikes, secondary action and mass picketing became a thing of the past and unions found themselves forced to moderate their strategies and tactics in dealing with employers. Labour market and pay flexibility were assisted by the Wages Act (1986), which reduced the role of Wages Councils to fix wage levels, and profit-related pay and decentralised pay bargaining procedures were encouraged.

Gradualism, and a popular cause, certainly assisted her union crusade. So too did an unplanned consequence of the early-1980s slump, the decline in manufacturing. Trade unions were traditionally strongest in those industries hardest hit by the recession – heavy engineering, docking, shipbuilding, transport – and they were weakest in those employment sectors growing in the 1980s, particularly high-tech companies and financial services. Trade union membership fell from 12 million to under 10 million in the recession, further reducing the unions' power, and their financial base. Defeat of the miners in 1984–85, the decisive union clash of her premiership, and one that dominated her personal attention throughout its prolonged agonies, was another death knell for militant unionism. Caution was thrown to the wind, and after 1987 her policy became 'an aggressive offensive designed to neuter the trade unions in the workplace and undermine collective bargaining as well as promote a flexible labour market based on individualistic values' [59 *p. 247*].

Again, trade union reform marked a sea-change in policy. The number of days lost in disputes during the 1980s was a quarter of the level in the strike-torn decade before. In 1990, the number of officially recorded strikes was at a 55-year low. The labour market was certainly freer in 1990 than in 1979, but still had a long way to go. Wage levels remained high by international standards, acting as a deterrent to fresh employment, while high house prices in the South and inadequate training, especially for young people, prevented business capitalising fully on growth opportunities because of difficulties in recruiting labour with requisite skills. Succeeding Conservative and Labour governments, despite rising public support for trade unions, and a widespread feeling that reform had gone far enough, continued to press for a more flexible labour market, and made sure that trade unions remained accountable to their members, while playing a reduced role in British public life.

The aim of reducing Britain's long-term relative economic decline, however, evident since 1900 and before, was only partly achieved. Productivity growth, a key indicator which should have risen with increased efficiency, grew in the mid-1980s but then fell back in the late 1980s. Productivity growth overall compared favourably with earlier decades, but international productivity comparisons show the 1980s British record in a mixed light. This is because, despite high growth rates, after consistently lagging behind many of her competitors in productivity growth in the past, Britain had a great deal of lost ground to make up even to achieve an equal level of productivity with many other European nations. Finally, it should be noted that even where the economic miracle existed, it was uneven. As Michael Porter has shown, renewal could be seen in certain sectors, such as in the clerical, oil, pharmaceutical, publishing, software, and financial sectors, and in certain areas, above all in the South-East. Any talk of an economic miracle must thus be heavily circumscribed [67 *p. 227*].

THE WELFARE STATE

Social policy, ironically, saw far less of an ideological thrust forward than was evident in the economic realm. Mrs Thatcher's social mission was equally clear-cut: roll back excessive state activity and bureaucracy and let individuals stand on their own two feet. Correlli Barnett, the influential right-of-centre historian who argued that the money Britain had invested in the NHS should have been invested in industry, and other authors had instilled in Mrs Thatcher and her acolytes a detestation of the 'dependency culture', where individual and family autonomy had been atrophied by creeping welfare statism. The project was thus to replace dependency with not just an enterprise, but also a 'self-help' culture.

Some areas did see lasting change, above all the encouragement for people to opt out of the welfare state. In 1980, enacting an idea mooted in Number Ten under Labour after 1974, council house tenants were given the right to buy their own house. Over one million families or individuals became homeowners. The 'assisted places scheme' allowed able children from less well-off backgrounds to secure means-tested places at the country's independent schools. In 1990, those over the age of 60 were given tax relief on private health insurance, in an attempt to reduce the burden on the NHS and to expand the private health sector.

Another theme was targeting help on the most deserving, which had been enthusiastically proposed by right-wing think tanks such as the Institute of Economic Affairs (IEA) for many years. Successive reforms of the social security system progressively tightened the eligibility rules for unemployment benefit. Means-testing was extended while payouts from insurance-based benefits were restricted, and the level of the popular universal benefit paid to parents (child benefit) was frequently frozen year on year.

The search for increasing efficiency and applying market disciplines in the NHS and the education system has been chronicled in some detail in Chapter 4. The NHS internal market gave GPs budgets and led to hospitals competing for patients. Similarly, social service departments were to become purchasers of care for their elderly and disabled populations. With the 1988 Housing Act, alternative landlords could take over individual council properties or whole estates with the agreement of the tenants. The provision for schools to 'opt out' of local authority control, which was provided by the 1988 Education Reform Act, enhanced parental choice over their children's education and devolved budgetary responsibility to the schools themselves. First the NHS, and then local government, were forced to put some services out to tender. 'Efficiency audits' became the order of the day: even grand figures like hospital consultants and university professors had to account for their spending of public money. Although these reforms achieved some decentralisation, state control was also enhanced through policies such as the introduction of a national curriculum, the abolition of the Inner London Education Authority, and the increase in central government control over university funding.

Howard Glennerster writes that 'taken together, this legislation was the biggest break with social policy tradition since 1945' [59 *p. 322*].

Nevertheless, it is often argued that social policy is an area in which the Thatcher government lacked its radical edge. Radical options, including a 'whole-hog' privatisation of the NHS, a refusal to give benefits to the unemployed unless they retrained or took alternative work, and education 'vouchers', where parents would have an entirely free hand in the choice of their child's school, were all ideas that the government considered, but dropped. Whereas the long-standing rate of state *increase* on welfare spending slowed, there was still a real rise in public spending on welfare by a fifth, with health and social security spending a third higher in real terms in 1990 than in 1979. The changes also came late in the day: very little welfare reform came until Mrs Thatcher's third administration, though the prescriptions had all been available since 1979. The reforms were then often enacted too quickly, and in some cases had to be funda-mentally altered. Some measures had unfortunate consequences: while the 'right to buy' policy increased owner-occupation to two-thirds of all households, the failure to address distortions in the hous-ing market, coupled with an overheated economy, produced the huge disparity in house prices country-wide which handicapped labour mobility. Over-inflated house prices meant that for many the endur-ing legacy of the Thatcher government's social policy was 'negative equity'. Boosts in numbers of students in higher education, from 535,000 to 710,000 during the 1980s, were not always well provided for. In terms of the quality of higher education, Kingsley Amis's old dictum might well have been fair comment: more will mean worse. Several of the reforms showed little take-up: only 70 schools opted out by 1991, while only a handful of tenants and estates chose to 'opt out' under the 1988 and 1989 Housing Acts.

Mrs Thatcher famously assured the electorate 'the NHS is safe in our hands' and the welfare state survived the Thatcher treatment. Thereafter, neither Conservative nor Labour government again seri-ously considered abolishing it, though the drive for greater efficiency, visibility and accountability, given impetus by Mrs Thatcher, all con-tinued unabated. Demographic change and technological advance, entailing an ever older population and ever more sophisticated and expensive treatments on offer, were as important in driving the search for efficiencies in the welfare state as ideology.

BRITAIN IN THE WORLD

If Mrs Thatcher was only partly successful in reducing Britain's rela-tive economic decline, she had more success in arresting Britain's decline as a world power, a fact of life since the end of the Second World War and the loss of the colonial empire. By the 1970s, Britain was being labelled the 'sick man of Europe', and in 1976 had been forced to go, cap in hand, to the International Monetary Fund to ask for financial help. The premiership of Callaghan did little to enhance Britain's standing in the world, despite Callaghan's experience as Foreign Secretary.

In contrast, Mrs Thatcher came to power in 1979 with no ministerial foreign policy experience. The Falklands War in 1982 altered her entire perception of her foreign policy role. Incensed by the invasion of the islands by the Argentinian Junta, she was determined that the invaders had to be removed. Her personal drive won her admirers, in Britain and abroad: the successful outcome, by no means a foregone conclusion, was a great personal victory for her. As Anthony Parsons wrote: 'the efficiency with which the military operation was concluded won widespread respect and British prestige rose to a higher level in the summer of 1982 than for many years' [58 *p. 158*].

The greatest boost to Britain's standing came on the intercontinental stage. Her relationship with Reagan (US President 1981–89) proved critical, not just in helping ensure US support for the British campaign in the Falklands, but in raising her standing among world leaders. Her support for the deployment of US Cruise and Pershing-2 missiles in Britain in the early 1980s leant support to Reagan's crusade to outspend the Soviet Union militarily. The Soviet Union accepted that it could not compete, without driving itself into the ground, and this acknowledgement encouraged it to look for other more peaceful ways forward. Gorbachev's easy relationship with Mrs Thatcher, forged in 1984 and 1985, allowed her to play a key brokering role between the leaders of the two superpowers. Not since Churchill's premiership in the early 1950s had Britain enjoyed so much respect in Washington and Moscow. The close relationship with the White House survived some difficult challenges, in particular the bombing of Libya by US planes based in Britain and the American invasion of Grenada. One of her last acts as Prime Minister, in November 1990, was to visit Paris to sign the treaty reducing conventional forces in Europe, thereby helping to bring the Cold War to a close. She had played an important part in bringing about this end: earlier Tory predecessors, notably Churchill and Macmillan, had sought the same end, without success.

The shift upwards in Britain's standing with the superpowers endured into the 1990s. Major forged a close personal link with Yeltsin, although this was not fully sustained by Blair. Major quickly re-established a close relationship with President Bush (1989–93), which had been lost in Mrs Thatcher's last two years. The Bush–Major relationship was cemented during the Gulf War in 1991, when Britain proved to be America's principal ally. Whereas Major and Clinton often fell out, principally over Ireland and Bosnia, Blair's relationship with Clinton approached that of Thatcher with Reagan, and reached a highpoint in the joint Anglo-American air strikes on Iraq in December 1998.

Mrs Thatcher was personally one of the most readily recognised world faces in the 1980s, and won high personal popularity in Eastern Europe as the Cold War was ending. She was not as well regarded in the European Community. Her early successes in reducing Britain's contribution to the EC budget won few friends, as did her hectoring manner and lack of warmth for things European. Her particular antipathy was to Germany, which damaged her relationship with Helmut Kohl. Though she gave strong support to the single market initiative and was persuaded to that end to sign up to the Single European Act, she was transparently uncomfortable with the movement towards greater political and economic union. She spent five years battling to prevent Britain joining the ERM before succumbing in October 1990. Few European leaders were sorry to see her fall a month later, and it cannot be said that she either established a clear British position on Europe, or that Britain's standing with her EC partners was any higher in 1990 than it had been in 1979. Nor did she help unite her own party behind an agreed position on Europe, which by the late 1980s had become the salient issue.

Mrs Thatcher was no better loved by her Commonwealth partners than by her EC counterparts. Although she helped pilot through a successful Rhodesian agreement, giving the former colony independence in 1980, she was renowned as being unsympathetic to the aspirations of black nations, while her contempt and refusal to support Commonwealth sanctions against South Africa excited widespread hostility among Commonwealth leaders. As with Europe, Britain was continually on the defensive instead of leading the offensive.

Mrs Thatcher's support, albeit reluctant, for the 1985 Anglo-Irish (Hillsborough) Agreement stands out in contrast to her general constitutional conservatism. The measure saw Dublin renounce claims over Northern Ireland, unless a majority in Ulster wanted it, but also saw the British accept, for the first time, Dublin's claim to a say in the running of Ulster. The Agreement stands out as an important milestone on the road to the political reform of the mid and late 1990s.

THE GOVERNMENT AND THE CONSTITUTION

Mrs Thatcher was not very interested in governing as a process; she was extremely interested in the outputs – the policies. Nevertheless, central government, and its local counterpart, did change between 1979 and 1990, and hence so too did the constitution. Minor changes occurred at the heart of government: some departments were broken up (Health and Social Security in 1988), while others re-merged (Trade and Industry in 1983). In addition, the Civil Service Department was abolished in 1981 and the Central Policy Review Staff ('think tank') in 1983, while the Prime Minister's office in Number Ten grew in size, although it fell a long way short of becoming a 'Prime Minister's Department', as some had urged her to create in 1982–84. Some commentators, like Peter Hennessy and Hugo Young, saw Mrs Thatcher adopting 'presidential traits'. On one level this was true: she did sideline Cabinet discussion more than her predecessors, and by the end she was relying disproportionately on the advice of two men, Charles Powell and Bernard Ingham, neither of them elected politicians. But following a familiar pattern (Lloyd George succeeded by Bonar Law, Churchill by Attlee), a strong Prime Minister (Thatcher) was followed by a more collegial one (Major). There was no long-term shift in power towards presidentialism, and one can confidently predict that Blair will be succeeded by a more collegial premier.

Neither is there much in the claim that Mrs Thatcher 'politicised' the civil service, by promoting those who were ideologically or personally sympathetic to her over the heads of those who were just as able but ideologically hostile. She certainly had a distaste for civil servants and regarded some, including several at the Treasury and Foreign Office, as cryptosocialists or 'defeatists'. But a 1986 independent Royal Institute of Public Administration report found her, rightly, to be guiltless of promoting 'right-wing' officials. What it did conclude was that she had a preference for 'action' civil servants, who were 'pro-active' and quick-thinking rather than cogitative and reactive.

The most striking change to central government came in outright staff reductions. Civil service numbers fell from 730,000 in 1979 to a postwar low of 562,000 by 1990. Much of the fall came in the 'blue-collar' civil service, industrial civil servants working mainly in the defence field. Another important change, initiated by Mrs Thatcher in the 'Next Steps' initiative of 1988, and continued by Major and Blair, was that the core civil service was to be more clearly identified with 'policy'. Other activities traditionally performed by central government were to be 'hived off', to be discharged either by agencies or the private sector. Local government changed too, even more dramatically than government at the centre. Kenneth Young believes 'of all Mrs Thatcher's confrontations with the institutions, that which she has fought with local government has been the most prolonged and is arguably the most significant of all' [*58 p. 124*]. In contrast to the long tradition of Conservative support for local government, she certainly had little respect or time for it. Neither did her Environment Secretaries; together they believed that public spending could never be brought down as long as the left-wing councils were spending money freely, and in 1979 local authority expenditure accounted for 28% of total government spending. To Mrs Thatcher, local government was wasteful, unaccountable and ultimately undesirable: it was thus ripe for reform. The details of the reforms can be found in Chapter 4: tight financial controls, 'tendering' of services hitherto provided by local government, opting out of local schools, sales of council houses – all undermined local authorities. 'Rate capping', whereby overspending local authorities were subjected to financial penalties imposed by Whitehall, came progressively into play: 18 local authorities (all but two Labour-controlled) were rate-capped in 1985–86. In 1986 the Greater London Council and six other Metropolitan Authorities were abolished and in 1989 the radical Community Charge ('poll tax') was introduced. Although designed to enhance further the accountability of local authorities to their local electorates, in practice it added further to the power of central government. Although the unpopular poll tax was swept aside in 1991, other Thatcherite reforms to local government remained in place. Indeed, Major accelerated the decline of local government autonomy, goaded on by Kenneth Clarke, a confessed sceptic about its value. Under New Labour, through policies such as the creation of an elected mayor for London, there is evidence that the trend to centralism is being reversed.

On a wider scale, Mrs Thatcher was not a constitutional reformer. She did not favour devolution or reform of the House of Lords. The Conservative Party's organisation was largely unchanged by her. She had far greater impact on the structure of the Liberal and Labour Parties than on the Tories. While the former was transmogrified into the Liberal Democrats, socialism in the latter, typified by Michael Foot (Labour leader 1980–83) was relegated to the outer margins. Neither did the Tory Party's ideology change much during her time in office: she began her premiership surrounded by 'wet' opponents around her Cabinet table, and she ended it surrounded by ideological enemies.

All three candidates for the succession in November 1990 were non-Thatcherites (though Major made some Thatcherite noises). The Parliamentary party became only marginally more 'Thatcherite' in the 1980s, though the 1992 general election, ironically after she had fallen, saw a big influx of 'Thatcher's children'.

Critics alleged that the judiciary became more political, the state less respectful of civil liberties, and the police more repressive, especially of ethnic minorities. Although there were some well-documented miscarriages of justice during the Thatcher years, it is also true that lawyers proved tough opponents of the Thatcher government's policies, proving that judicial independence was alive and well. The ending of trade union rights at the Government's Communication Headquarters (GCHQ) at Cheltenham in 1984 is perhaps the best example of excessive state power trampling on individual rights, and through cases such as the celebrated attempt to ban ex-MI5 Officer Peter Wright's book *Spycatcher* under the Official Secrets Act, the government established a reputation for an obsession with secrecy. Excessive use of force by the police may have increased in the 1980s, but if so, it did not stop notified crime rising by 60% between 1979 and 1990.

THE ESTABLISHMENT AND VALUES

The establishment at large did not like Mrs Thatcher. Even the Queen was said to find her uncongenial. She alienated the professions – lawyers, doctors, university teachers – by, in their view, meddling in their affairs. She was detested by many in the media, except for a group of right-wing writers like Paul Johnson, Woodrow Wyatt and John O'Sullivan. The cultural elite had almost universal contempt for her, with playwright Harold Pinter being one of the more vociferous voices. Her own university, Oxford, humiliated her by turning down a proposal to give her an honorary degree. Peers in the House of Lords generally disliked her, while her own Parliamentary party, although generally respecting her, offered her little or no affection, before ultimately rejecting her.

Thatcherism made as little impact on the nation's values as she herself did on the establishment. As Ivor Crewe put it succinctly: 'quite simply, there has been no Thatcherite transformation of attitudes or behaviour among the British people. If anything, the British have edged further away from Thatcherite positions as the decade ... progressed' [58 *p. 241*]. A whole army of opinion poll and statistical data concur that the public at large had a distaste for Thatcherite ideals:

they were happy to pay higher taxes if it meant better public services and welfare, and favoured more compassionate, caring policies and rhetoric. Survey data and statistics can be infinitely open to interpretation, but it can nevertheless be asserted that if Mrs Thatcher's intention was to alter the mindset of the British public from welfarism to enterprise, then on this measure at least, she failed.

Britain certainly became a more unequal society during the 1980s, although it is likely that with technological and industrial change, this polarisation would have occurred to some extent without Mrs Thatcher at the helm. The number reliant on income support and one-parent benefits increased during the 1980s from 3.4 million to over 5.5 million. The proportion of families with no full-time worker rose from 27% to 37% over the decade. In 1979, the richest 10% of the population had 20.6% of the nation's wealth, and the poorest 10% had 4.3%. By 1991 the figures had altered to 26.1% and 2.9%, a tremendous contrast. As against this, general prosperity grew considerably, reflected in the proportion of families with telephones rising from 62% to 85%, and those with central heating from 54% to 77%. If the Thatcher premiership teaches us one thing, it is the folly of generalisation.

7 · THATCHERISM IN HISTORY

Every Prime Minister, every political leader, has his or her career picked over and interpreted by analysts and historians. Judgements become easier to make the further in time the period under consideration is from the present day, and the less controversial the leader. The merits of Elizabeth I as English monarch (1558–1603) continue to divide historians; but few leaders arouse such passion, both at the time and subsequently, as Mrs Thatcher.

Seven perspectives will be offered on Mrs Thatcher's period as party leader (1975–90) and Prime Minister (1979–90). In each case, specific exponents of aspects of the interpretation will be highlighted, so that readers who wish to pursue particular lines further can do so. This chapter concludes with the authors' own interpretation, which can be seen as either an eighth perspective, or an amalgam of the other seven. The perspectives are as follows:

- The right-wing perspective, focusing on the academic, Shirley Letwin.
- A centre-left Conservative ('wet') critique, associated with the former Tory minister, Ian Gilmour.
- The centralisation ('strong state') critique, offered by political scientist, Andrew Gamble and journalist, Simon Jenkins.
- A left of centre critique, drawn from various writers with historian Kenneth Morgan of particular interest.
- A contemporary historian's perspective, drawn from commentator, Dennis Kavanagh.
- The historical determinist thesis, proposed by academic, Ben Pimlott.
- An historian's perspective, taken from historian Eric Evans.

THE RIGHT-WING PERSPECTIVE

There can be no doubt that Mrs Thatcher's greatest supporters can be found among those conventionally referred to as the 'right wing' of the Tory Party. Although die-hard right-wing radicals may argue that Thatcherism did not go far enough in breaking with the perceived failures of the past, the more mainstream right wing are generous with their praise and suggest that, on the whole, Thatcherism enjoyed significant success.

True Thatcher loyalists make bold claims for Mrs Thatcher, commonly arguing that she was the most effective peacetime twentieth-century premier (upstaging Lloyd George, 1916–22, and Attlee, 1945–51). They see Mrs Thatcher personally as utterly eclipsing all others in the success of her premiership: lieutenants such as Geoffrey Howe and Nigel Lawson are accorded minor roles, and are blamed for her downfall and letting in the 'weak' John Major as her successor.

Supporters like Shirley Letwin judge the principal Thatcherite achievement to be the reversing of the 'socialist consensus' [61 p. 316], inaugurated by the postwar Attlee government and adhered to since by governments of both left and right. Thatcherism achieved, Letwin argues, the restoration of the 'vigorous virtues' of the individual (including self-sufficiency, moral virtue and a spirit of adventure) and also engineered a 'paradigm shift in the relation between the government and the governed' [61 p. 47]. Thatcherism is thus a 'form of practical politics devoted to achieving certain concrete results in Britain at the end of the twentieth century' [61 p. 39].

This view praises the broad privatisation thrust of her governments, which restored vitality to the economy by replacing state subsidies to ailing industries by successful industrial enterprises earning profit, which themselves facilitated tax cuts. Competition replaced state monopoly, boosting efficiency. Although some on the radical right believe that privatisation was a missed opportunity as the bulk of shares ended up with institutional investors, loyalists argue that privatisation did spread share ownership to many new and often first-time shareholders, thus entrenching 'popular capitalism'. New share owners became new home owners through the sale of council houses, thus promoting the 'vigorous virtues' and boosting family cohesion by allowing families to pass down property and values from one generation to the next. Letwin is keen to stress that 'Thatcherism is not, and cannot possibly be understood as, an economic policy' [61 p. 117]. Because the policy tools changed, from monetarism to exchange rate management, one should speak not of a single Thatcherite economic policy, but of a Thatcherite attitude to economics, including a commitment to price stability and the promotion of savings, but all with the avoidance of direct economic management. Thatcherites rejected the postwar notion that problems in the economy are best cured by government interference. The Thatcherite mission was thus to provide a framework for individuals to pursue their own interests as free as possible from government intervention.

Another manifestation of the Thatcherite bolstering of the individual and the onslaught on powerful interests, which interfered with the free market, came in the government's assault on overmighty trade union power. Here, the radical and moderate right tend to unite in praise of the government's record. The legislation that was introduced was intended 'fundamentally to restore and clarify the government's authority to rule' [61 *p. 132*]. Since 1945, governments of both left and right had allowed trade union power to rise to excessive levels, and in the 1970s the unions had aroused popular ire by challenging the authority of the British State. The trade union legislation and direct attack on union action, notably during the miners' strike in 1984–85, were unavoidable:

> In taking such 'tough' measures on trade unions, the Thatcher government was answering a widespread and deeply felt public demand to be liberated from a tyranny which, apart from its effect on employers, had made it impossible for Britain to know from one day to the next what stoppage would produce chaos in their daily life. [61 *p. 157*]

Supporters praise Thatcherite policy towards local government because local authorities were seen to be bastions of municipal socialism, whose spending of public money had run out of control. Reducing their financial independence was thus vital if Mrs Thatcher was to achieve her objective of reducing overall government spending, of which local authority expenditure formed such a large part. Local government successes also came with the 'contracting out' of services, formerly provided by local authorities, to the private sector, thus promoting efficiency through competition. Although the poll tax may have failed in practice, despite the claims of its detractors it was an attempt to enhance local autonomy and local authority accountability, which in turn Mrs Thatcher hoped would force authorities to reduce their taxes and thus their spending. In short, 'local government was not an ancient bastion of local autonomy and liberty: and the Thatcher government's attack on it was the very opposite of an attempt to centralise' [61 *p. 159*]. The reduction in size of central government, carried out by a series of civil service cuts and by 'contracting out' various tasks to private operators, was part of this keen Thatcherite zeal to reduce state bureaucracy and bolster the private sector. What remained in the public sector was subjected to new managerial efficiencies. This thrust was informed in part by 'public choice' theorists such as Gordon Tullock and William Niskanen who argued that state bureaucracies would have every incentive to increase in size and little incentive to reduce.

Letwin is not so fulsome in her praise of the government's social policy, which most supporters acknowledge was an unfinished aspect of the Thatcher revolution. The radical right are more critical, claiming that her social policy lacked vision. She failed to overcome vested interests and allowed incrementalism to take the place of radical reform. The broad Thatcherite thrusts of social policy were first, ensuring greater personal responsibility (an assault on the so-called 'dependency culture', in which the welfare state was seen as eroding individual and family initiative by the intervention of state support and bureaucracy), and secondly, ensuring greater value for money and efficiency. Some reforms assisted in these directions: the 1983 Griffiths Report into the NHS, for example, was followed by the introduction of more managerial efficiency and 'contracting out'. The internal market and GP fundholding were also introduced to increase efficiency and to ensure NHS resources were used to best effect.

In education, Thatcherism was directed against the poor standards and the 'progressive education' disease, which impoverished children. Schools were being weakened by a culture of mediocrity, low expectations, union-minded teachers and control by local government bureaucracy. Parents also suffered by being denied choice, a problem exacerbated by Labour's emasculation of grammar schools and their replacement by comprehensives. Although the education voucher scheme proved politically unacceptable, the 'assisted places scheme' allowed parents from low-income families to receive the benefits of independent schooling and achieved similar parental choice objectives to the voucher scheme [61 *p. 239*]. The 1988 Education Reform Act, with its creation of 'grant maintained' schools which had 'opted out' of local authority control, allowed these schools freedom from the stranglehold of local government oversight. The National Curriculum was seen as 'the way to promote the vigorous virtues and to make Britain a flourishing nation' [61 *p. 263*], but in the end it was hijacked by the educational establishment. There are few blandishments for Mrs Thatcher's policy towards higher education (in which Letwin worked) as the policy saw 'education as a means to economic success' [61 *p. 275*] and diminished the importance of academic study for its own sake.

In the realm of foreign and defence policy, loyalists typically see Mrs Thatcher as transforming Britain from 'the sick man of Europe', marginalised on the world stage because of its inability to govern itself, into a proud and self-confident player in the international arena. Mrs Thatcher's own personal fortitude during the Falklands crisis, her support for Britain's upgraded nuclear deterrent, and her influential personal relations with Presidents Reagan of the USA and Gorbachev of the USSR, are milestones along the road in the transformation of Britain's international standing. Letwin praises Mrs Thatcher's early successes in reducing the British contribution to the EC budget, and the adoption of the Single European Act, which was seen essentially as a way to advance the free market within Europe. Loyalists are generally supportive of her increasingly Euro-sceptical attitude from the mid to late 1980s, when she saw the dangers of the EC's centralist political ambitions, and they applaud her 1988 Bruges anti-federalist speech. The radical right give her later Eurosceptical stance strong support, but only regret that she did not adopt it earlier. Her failure to reject the Single European Act and resist ERM membership are seen as disastrous, as both were simply not in Britain's interest. To loyalists, snobbery, both intellectual and social, and more than a touch of male chauvinism account for the criticism Mrs Thatcher received while premier and subsequently. She also aroused antipathy by her assault on pressure groups and vested interests, whether the trade unions, doctors, lawyers, academics or the Church. Loyalists point out that the very extent of the change she enacted in such a brief time was also bound to arouse ire. Although the radical right would play down the change that actually took place, they would find much to commend in Letwin's conclusion that 'the true effect of Thatcherism on British political thinking' [61 *p. 316*] is illustrated by the changes she brought to the Labour Party, which came to accept most of her reforms. In short, 'Thatcherism has changed the intellectual agenda of political discourse' [61 *p. 315*].

THE CENTRE-LEFT CONSERVATIVE ('WET') CRITIQUE

The 'wets' offered the most voluminous and sustained critique of Thatcherism throughout the eleven and a half years of her government. Arguably, the faction triumphed over her, as by 1990 her Cabinet contained barely a single Thatcher loyalist, and was full of pragmatic centre or centre-left ministers such as Douglas Hurd, Chris Patten and John Gummer. This is the tendency in the party which has been in the ascendant since Stanley Baldwin was Prime Minister in the interwar years, and of which every postwar premier until Thatcher – Churchill, Eden, Macmillan, Home and Heath – was an exponent.

This stance has also been identified as 'One Nation' Conservatism, after the coining of the phrase 'one nation' by the nineteenth-century Tory leader, Benjamin Disraeli. 'One Nation' Tories believe that the Conservative Party should appeal to all classes in Britain, not just the better off or the strong, and should adopt policies to improve the lot of all sectors in society.

The most articulate single figure from the Tory left is Ian Gilmour, whose book *Dancing with Dogma* [16] sets out a detailed analysis and criticism of the Thatcher years.

Only a few of the more pungent criticisms need be recollected here: one of the greatest complaints undoubtedly concerns Thatcherite economic policy. For Gilmour, monetarism, the 'economic dogma' at the 'core' of Thatcherism [16 *p. 9*], caused 'quite unnecessarily, far and away the worst recession since the war' [16 *p. 25*]. As a result, unemployment doubled during 1979–81, causing widespread poverty and misery, and between one-quarter and one-fifth of manufacturing industry was wiped out. Lasting economic damage was caused and the policy in her early years was 'simply a failure' [16 *p. 68*]. When the policy switched to exchange rate stability after 1983 under Lawson, it 'combined the worst features of monetarism and Keynesianism' [16 *p. 61*], allowing unemployment to spiral with excessive demand in the economy. The 1988 Budget tax cuts were 'economic folly' giving 40% of tax cuts to the richest 5% of the population. The economy became greatly overheated, for which Lawson was allowed by Thatcherites to take the blame, and the ensuing slump caused more widespread suffering. The overall economic record was 'a miserable performance' [16 *p. 69*] and only the huge advantages of North Sea oil disguised the extent of the damage. Indicatively for a 'One Nation' Tory, the poor were neglected: 'the rich got richer and the poor got poorer' [16 *p. 113*]. As a result of the pursuit of economic dogma, unemployment was allowed to rise needlessly (the extent disguised by the government 'fiddling' the figures), and an 'underclass' grew greatly in size. The so-called 'Thatcher economic miracle' was a myth, the creation of the government propaganda machine.

Thatcherite social policy is similarly castigated. Even if radicals see Thatcherite social reforms as too little too late, the faction at least accepts that the reforms were aimed in the right direction. Not so for the centre-left, who believe that Thatcherite dogma prevented the government seeing the key problem in the NHS: under-funding. The late 1980s' health reforms were prompted by 'pseudo free market liberalism' [16 *p. 157*], the policies were insufficiently tested and the creation of paperwork diverted money and time away from patient care. The

reforms were an 'unnecessary, though convenient distraction from the
... chronic underfunding' of the NHS, producing a 'more fragmented,
less altruistic and probably more expensive' service [16 *pp. 160–1*].
Free market dogma gone wild was responsible for a slate of other
social policy failures. Education reforms demoralised the teaching
profession, while 'opting out' of local authority control made a non-
sense of rational planning and meeting of pupil needs: 'Thatcherites
see the world as a prolonged series of groceries whereby people
choose education from Tesco and local government from Sainsbury's
... this view is fallacious' [16 *p. 170*]. Introducing market forces into
higher education 'jeopardised the worldwide reputation of British
universities' [16 *p. 165*], while 200 British professors left for the USA
from 1983 to 1988 as part of the government-provoked 'brain drain'.
Housing policy did not allow sufficient funding for new council
houses, contributing to a rise in homelessness. Needless hardship was
also caused by the deterioration of the social security system.

Like many in the centre/centre-left of the Tory party, Gilmour is
scornful of Mrs Thatcher's European policy. There was no long-term
policy, but an increasingly negative stance and a series of minor victories fought in aggressive style which played to an audience at home
but did not win friends abroad nor serve Britain's long-term interests.

Gilmour is not without praise for aspects of Thatcherite policy – he
is, after all, a life-long Tory. In common with many on the right, Gilmour sees trade union reform as 'Thatcher's most important achievement' [16 *p. 79*] and the miners' strike campaign was conducted 'bril-
liantly' by the government [16 *p. 91*]. Gilmour soon parts company
with the radicals, however, by proclaiming privatisation a 'Thatcherite triumph' [16 *p. 104*] which 'has attracted admiration both here
and abroad' [16 *p. 93*]. (Nevertheless, he has several reservations
about the privatisation programme, echoing the standard complaint
that monopoly status was often retained, and he further claims that
the rich benefited rather than 'the people', and later privatisation, e.g.
Royal Ordnance, was driven solely by dogma.) In foreign affairs, Mrs
Thatcher deserves praise for the settlement of the Rhodesia problem
in 1979–80, for the conduct of the Falklands War, the Anglo-Irish
Agreement and her handling of the invasion of Kuwait in 1990. But
overall, she squandered the opportunities for enhancing Britain's
heightened world standing after the low points of the 1970s, such as
the IMF loan: 'because of economic failure, Britain's heightened stat-
ure was not matched by increased British power' [16 *p. 266*].

THE CENTRALISATION ('STRONG STATE') CRITIQUE

In contrast with the previous perspectives, this critique does not seek to assess Thatcherite policies from a specific point on the political spectrum, but rather focuses on a particular charge against the Thatcher governments: the centralisation of government power. The irony of Thatcherite policies promoting *laissez-faire* and anti-statism while at the same time concentrating power in a strong central government has been discussed by two principal commentators, Andrew Gamble [44] and Simon Jenkins [53; 54].

Gamble first aired his thesis during the 1980s, suggesting that a strong state was required to enable the Thatcher government to roll back the government sector. Within central government, Parliament was by-passed and the executive, boosted by the large Thatcherite electoral victories, became predominant. Within the executive, power was concentrated with the Prime Minister at Number Ten, with the Cabinet, like the House of Commons, becoming little more than a rubber stamp. Local government was progressively by-passed and emasculated, notably through the introduction of rate capping (1984) and the abolition of the GLC and the other metropolitan authorities (1986), and the cumulative effect was 'a major shift in the balance of the constitution between local and central government' [44 *p. 240*].

This in itself demonstrated the inability of the British constitution to provide a check on modern executive power and Larry Siedentop has suggested that the ease with which Mrs Thatcher enacted these changes was, to a large degree, the result of changes she promoted in Britain's social structure. Siedentop argues that since the eighteenth century it was assumed that liberties not guaranteed by political institutions would be protected by social structure. A Parliament dominated by a wealthy, land-owning class, keen to keep control of the localities itself, would serve well to restrict any extension of executive power. In the absence of a codified constitution, the checks on executive power were thus 'informal' and relied on 'deference and a social hierarchy to limit the growth of state power' [72 *p. 88*]. However, Mrs Thatcher accelerated social change, favouring and enlarging the middle class at the expense of aristocratic values and thus helped to destroy the informal checks on excessive executive power that had hitherto operated. In Siedentop's view: 'Thatcher has completed the destruction of the informal supports which an aristocratic social structure provided for British liberty' [72 *p. 99*].

Pluralism, which hitherto had seen power shared across a wide variety of bodies, was progressively eroded along with civil liberties. Trade union autonomy, for example, was severely constrained: it was at Mrs Thatcher's personal insistence, against the advice of the Foreign Secretary and the Cabinet Secretary, that trade unions were banned at GCHQ. The police had their powers greatly strengthened to deal with the growing public disorder. 'Policing took on a more repressive character as those opposed to the Thatcher government came to be stigmatised as the "enemies within"' [44 *p. 242*]. Critics of the state, whether leakers or protesters, were hounded by a government obsessed with secrecy, and which failed to draw a true distinction between the interests of the British State and the interests of the Thatcher government. Repression was especially evident against black communities. The result of the Thatcherite period was the advent of 'two nation' politics, where the majority were given greater physical security and economic prospects while the minority of the poor and disadvantaged were repressed and made more dependent upon the state [44 *pp. 249–54*].

Simon Jenkins argues in a similar vein that 'the Thatcher decade saw the most intensive period of nationalisation since the Attlee government' of 1945–50 [53 *p. 18*]. In 1979, the 'commanding heights' of the public sector were still 'plural, disparate and largely self-governing' [53 *p. 18*]. By 1990, the public sector (and much of the private sector) had been subjected to far greater central government powers and controls, pulling off a movement to *dirigisme* more all-embracing than anything a Labour government would have dared contemplate.

Jenkins's thesis bristles with examples of this accretion of central government power. The police were nationalised, with local police authorities amalgamated under new committees under the aegis of the Home Secretary. Budgets, staffing and spending were all controlled from Whitehall. Schools were similarly subjected to central diktat, with central government controlling not only what was taught in the classroom but also examinations and teachers' pay. An intrusive central government also damaged the quality of university life, and diminished the professional relationship of trust between patient and doctor, and hospital and community. In local government, rate capping and the uniform business rate fixed by the Treasury represented a 'drastic' extension of the fiscal power of the British Cabinet, which was of course dominated by the Prime Minister.

Jenkins's pen is at its sharpest when describing the proclaimed flagship of Thatcherite anti-statism: privatisation. The industries and services were never properly denationalised, with the State retaining significant shareholdings in most 'privatised' concerns. The new form of oversight, regulators, lacked any guiding philosophy: the result was that regulators both lacked teeth and had no formal accountability to

Parliament. In conclusion, Jenkins cites the words of the Labour minister and thinker, Douglas Jay, in 1939: 'the gentleman in Whitehall really does know better' – it took half a century for the Thatcher government to bring that belief to reality [53 *p. 18*].

A LEFT OF CENTRE CRITIQUE

The left have a problem with placing Thatcherism. The Marxist left find the task easiest: root-and-branch condemnation can be found in the writing of Stuart Hall [45]. To Marxists, Thatcherism was the most nakedly pro-capitalist Conservative government since the war, deliberately emasculating organised labour and hounding the far left, both overtly and covertly, while rewarding the strong, able and young, resulting in a widening gap between rich and poor, North and South and the haves and the have-nots.

A similar theme, although not taken to the extremes of Marxists, is pursued by mainstream old-style Labour critics. Many on the traditional left repudiate Mrs Thatcher for trying to advance capitalism at the expense of boosting inequality. We have already seen protests against the rise in inequality from the Tory left, but the Labour left take the criticism considerably further than the likes of Ian Gilmour. Such a view can be found in the writings of historian Kenneth Morgan. For Morgan, the growing gulf between the South and Midlands that revelled in a newfound prosperity and an impoverished North-East, Merseyside and Scotland, all of which rejected Thatcherism electorally, is a fundamental criticism. The poor became poorer: after six years of Thatcher governments, Morgan observes, the poorest 20% received less than the 5.9% of national income that they received in 1979. Monetarism did not boost long-term growth, nor did it conquer inflation, which rose towards the end of Mrs Thatcher's time in office. The side-effects of Thatcherite economics included levels of unemployment unknown since the 1930s, another key factor in the increase in inequality and a far cry from the goal of full employment proclaimed by Attlee's Labour administration of 1945–51, still considered a key objective by many left-wingers.

Privatisation did not benefit consumers at large, who were not the beneficiaries of popular capitalism. Rather, it was the corporate sector and higher income groups who milked the 'privatisation dividend'. This boosted Conservative support among these groups, but also boosted inequality. It was also the better-off who benefited most from Tory trade union bashing, which swung the balance of power between trade unions and employers too far in the latter's direction.

Furthermore, while the well-off were rewarded with underpriced shares and massive cuts in the higher tax rate, the poor suffered from the downgrading of standard benefits: the link between the state pension and earnings was broken in 1983 so it failed to keep pace with increasing salaries and Child Benefit decreased by 21% in real terms between 1979 and 1990. Housing policy produced further inequality as better-off homeowners gained through mortgage interest taxation relief, wheras council house tenants were squeezed through the raising of rents and the sale of council houses that were not replaced.

Inequality was also promoted in social policy. In education the left saw the 'assisted places scheme' as promoting elitism and condemned the allocation of public money to a select few rather than using it for the benefit of all, through investment in the cash-starved state education system. The NHS was also desperately short of money and inequality was furthered through the promotion of private healthcare for the well-off, notably through tax breaks for the elderly, rather than using higher taxation to provide the desperately needed cash for investment in the health service.

In conclusion, Andrew Gamble, from similar persuasion, argues that Thatcherism was good 'for financial Britain, for multinational Britain, for rural Britain, for share-owning and upper-income Britain, but not so good for working-class Britain, for manufacturing Britain, for trade-union Britain, for unemployed Britain, for inner-city Britain or for single-parent Britain' [44 *p. 25*].

The social democrat or New Labour left have the greatest problems with Thatcherism. Tony Blair owes much to her political legacy. Not only did she destroy the old-style leftism of Michael Foot, Arthur Scargill and Ken Livingstone, but her policies of reducing the role of central government, boosting individualism (at the expense of organised interests) and promoting a vigorous national self-interest have been directly copied by the Labour Prime Minister since 1997. He owed more to her than to James Callaghan or even Harold Wilson. Some commentators even saw a similar presidential style, an impatience with those in their own party who disagree, and a reliance on a hard-hitting Press Secretary (Bernard Ingham and Alistair Campbell) to 'get the message across'. Criticisms levelled by New Labour at Mrs Thatcher could highlight her constitutional conservatism, an overly belligerent attitude towards the EU, and an over-reliance on the free market leading to insufficient regard for the plight of the under-privileged, an issue New Labour's 'Third Way' is designed to address.

A CONTEMPORARY HISTORIAN'S PERSPECTIVE

A different order of critique comes from Dennis Kavanagh, whose book, *Thatcherism and British Politics* [56], was the first serious attempt to fit the work of the Thatcher governments into a historical perspective. Kavanagh later wrote:

> Historians are likely to regard the Attlee government, which laid down the main planks of postwar political consensus, and the post-1979 Thatcher governments which, aided by events, have presided over the breakdown of much of the postwar political consensus as the two book-ends of postwar Britain. So I see postwar British politics between the late 1940s and the 1980s being, as it were, made and unmade by the Attlee and the Thatcher governments. [*57 p. 17*]

To Kavanagh, the doctrine of the postwar consensus is key. Laid down by the postwar Labour government (1945–51), it consisted of five main planks: the commitment to maintain full employment; conciliation or acceptance of trade unions having a right to be consulted in affairs of the realm; the mixed economy, with the state having a large role in both ownership of industry and intervention; the welfare state providing a free and universal service; and finally, a belief in using economic, regional and social policy to promote equality. Kavanagh argues that these policies were pursued by both Labour and Conservative governments until the 1970s. Mrs Thatcher's historic role was to dismantle the planks, either in their entirety or, as in the case of the welfare state, in part. The notion of the consensus has been variously contested, but nevertheless has been widely accepted as an important interpretative framework for comprehending Mrs Thatcher's historical role.

THE HISTORICAL DETERMINIST THESIS

This thesis, which has been principally propounded by Ben Pimlott, seeks to look beyond the shores of Britain at what was happening in other countries. Similar policies were being enacted, whether in the United States or in Germany, to improve the supply-side of the economy. Was Thatcherism merely the British expression of a world-wide move to strengthen capitalism at the expense of organised labour? Supporters of the determinist view also point to pre-1979 antecedents of Thatcherism, notably Heath's first phase of government policies from 1970 to 1972 and the policies of the Callaghan government from 1976 to 1979, notably the limits to public sector pay increases.

While agreeing with Dennis Kavanagh that the Thatcher administrations saw important changes to the Keynesian postwar consensus, determinists stress the unimportance of Mrs Thatcher's leadership. They argue that the tide of history was thus already turning against consensus policies in many key areas as the 1970s drew to a close, and thus the victor of the 1979 election was, to a large degree, an historical irrelevance. Pimlott concludes that, with the probable exceptions of the increase in mass unemployment, and the diminution of the power of local government, many of the policies from 1979–90 'would have happened anyway, albeit with a different rhetoric, under Labour' [65 *p. 15*]. If this school of thought is right, then far too much attention has been given to Mrs Thatcher personally: she was not the architect of the historic changes of 1979–90, but history's handmaiden.

AN HISTORIAN'S PERSPECTIVE

All of the judgements expressed so far have been contemporary. The thesis of the prolific historian of eighteenth- and nineteenth-century Britain, Eric Evans, offers a valuable new perspective. Evans, writing at the end of the 1990s, also believes 'enough time has passed since the fall to make at least a preliminary evaluation of both Thatcher and the legacy of Thatcherism' [43 *p. 115*]. Such a long-haul perspective from one deeply versed in earlier history is invaluable.

Evans believes that the (apparently) widely-held view that Mrs Thatcher was a strong, successful leader who 'turned Britain around' is wrong: instead, he sees her as a 'damaging and divisive failure' [43 *p. 115*]. The albeit unintended consequence of her premiership was to make Britain 'less tolerant, more greedy and far less humane' [43 *p. 121*]. As a leader, she lacked any real historical sense of perspec-. tive. Her talk of the virtue of 'Victorian values' was risible, based on a most selective understanding of Victorian society: 'she entirely failed to notice ... that what might be termed the long century of growing state responsibility, dating roughly from 1830 to 1970, was fuelled in significant part by the need to control and moderate brute capitalism' [43 *p. 124*]. She ignored rationalism and empiricalism, and was driven by an ideology as insensitive as Bolshevism had been at the start of the century. Though there were some positive benefits, such as an aggregate increase in prosperity, yet 'the list of those things Thatcherism attacked or demeaned is far longer: welfare, the power of the state to improve people's lives, the professional ethic of service, local government, trade unions, the notion of community, Europe'. Evans's conclusion? 'Britain by the late 1980s had become a more grasping, greedy and mean-spirited society. Hers is a legacy to be lived down' [43 *p. 124*].

CONCLUSION: THATCHER AND THATCHERISM IN HISTORY

When formulating conclusions, it is important to distinguish comments on Mrs Thatcher herself, and on Thatcherism, or her governments' policies. She herself was a remarkable lady, of quite exceptional energy, courage and single-mindedness. She forced the pace of change that was underway already, and gave it a particular English 'gloss'. There is much to commend the words of Lord Blake, the quintessential Conservative historian:

> Margaret Thatcher's place in history is assured; the first woman to be prime minister, the first since Palmerston to win three successive general elections, the longest continuous holder of the office since Lord Liverpool. ... She was on the British political scene a giant among pygmies. She was one of the two greatest Conservative prime ministers in the 20th Century and one of the half dozen greatest prime ministers of all parties and all times. [Quoted in 67 *p. 222*]

But such highly-charged, Olympian judgements also overlook Mrs Thatcher's personal limitations. She excelled at some of the qualities of leadership, above all energy, guts, oratory and defining a strategic direction, but she was weak on mobilising support behind that direction. She was also weak at picking ministers and advisors: only her 1981 reshuffle can be judged a significant success. She was poor at retaining ministers, falling out with the vast majority of Thatcherites so that not a single 'true believer' stood in a powerful position around her Cabinet table in November 1990. She did not secure the succession. The care and warmth she showed her own circle in Number Ten was not translated to the Conservative Party in Parliament. She came to believe her own propaganda, and made the fatal error of relying on fewer and fewer people, by the end just two, Ingham and Powell. She had little respect for, or understanding of, constitutional convention or indeed democracy. She treated Cabinet as a means to her ends, and had little time for either Parliament or local democracy. She became obsessive about two policies that dragged her down: anti-Eurofederalism, and the poll tax. Properly managed, she could have built coalitions behind both positions, especially by allowing tactical concessions. She fell because she failed to notice she had not carried her supporters with her.

All Prime Ministers are, to some degree, dependent on luck. She enjoyed good luck in abundance. She was fortunate to come to power when the Keynesian social democratic consensus had become discredited, and when she had a set of policy prescriptions, worked up by think tanks and academics over 30 years, which were there for the taking. She was fortunate to face a Labour Party led by Michael Foot (1980–83) and to coincide with the creation of the SDP, ensuring a large third party vote, and helping her win large majorities of 41–43% of the popular vote. She was also fortunate to have clear enemies at home (the trade unions and militant left) and abroad (the Soviet Union and Argentinian Junta). North Sea oil helped fill the Treasury coffers at a critical time. But good leaders not only create, but capitalise on their luck. This she did with great aplomb. Overall, we judge Mrs Thatcher as a great leader, with great flaws.

A similar mixed verdict can be made about her government. We agree with Dennis Kavanagh that hers was one of the three great reforming administrations of the century (alongside the Liberals in 1906–14 and Labour in 1945–51). A detailed assessment of her policies can be found in Chapter 6, but to summarise, although she fell far short of creating an economic miracle and reversing Britain's decline, as well as failing to achieve a change in popular consciousness from dependency to an enterprise culture, her achievements were nevertheless impressive. A measure of the success of a government is how many of the reforms endure. The balance between the public and the private sectors has been shifted irreversibly (at least in the foreseeable future) towards the latter. Trade unions have been modernised: they are more accountable, and co-operative with the goals of business; British industry (which has survived) is more outward-looking and competitive internationally; and management (in both public and private sectors) is of higher quality. Vested interests, including the professions, have had a long-overdue shake-up. More people were encouraged to become 'stake-holders' in the country's wealth, most importantly through house purchase. Britain enjoys a higher standing on the world stage, albeit as an appendage to the United States.

The weaknesses of the government were again several. It failed to improve the democratic quality of life in Britain, and in some respects impoverished it. Changes in the economy went only skin-deep in some areas, especially in training and education. The government's welfare reforms came too late and were insufficiently thought through. Perhaps most damagingly, the government too often appeared to be acting in the interests of well-off, white males in England, while showing little concern for the fate of those afflicted by economic policy, most notably the unemployed. This was perhaps the inevitable consequence of her deliberate attempts to widen inequality in the belief that greater rewards for success and less cushioning of failure would act as an incentive to effort and enterprise.

So, what of Britain under Thatcher? A Britain less equal with a more powerful central government, but a Britain more economically efficient with union militancy curbed; a Britain with higher unemployment and inflation not yet tamed, but a Britain where more people owned their own shares and their own homes; and a Britain less popular among Europe's leaders, but with a rejuvenated 'special relationship' across the Atlantic; a Britain respected on the world stage. And finally a lady. Although she demonstrated the political courage and determination of a great leader, her record testifies to just how fine a line can exist between determination and obstinacy. By 1990 her stubbornness in certain policy areas had become too much. With the government embattled and desperately unpopular, although she was not for turning, the rest of her party were.

PART FOUR: DOCUMENTS

DOCUMENT 1   DISCREDITING THE LABOUR
                      GOVERNMENT

*Dating from the summer of 1978, this poster, a Saatchi and Saatchi creation,
was highly effective in highlighting Britain's economic problems and laying
the blame squarely on the Labour government.*

H. Young, [76], on plates between pp. 176 and 177.

DOCUMENT 2   HUGO YOUNG: THE EC BUDGET
                      AGREEMENT OF 30 MAY 1980

*By May 1980, the issue of Britain's excessive contribution to the EC budget
was nearing crisis point as Mrs Thatcher had already rejected several offers
from her European partners, claiming that the rebates were not enough. After
a Foreign Ministers' Meeting in Brussels, Gilmour and Carrington returned
with an agreement for Mrs Thatcher's approval. This document should be
compared with Mrs Thatcher's own account in Document 3.*

The Foreign Secretary and his lugubrious colleague, Gilmour, returned from Brussels pleased with what they had achieved. ... Their leader was less impressed. From the moment they set foot at Chequers to acquaint her with their triumph, she insisted that it was an unacceptable disaster. On Monday it adjourned to full Cabinet. Still the prime minister continued the fight. To several of those present it became apparent that she was ready, indeed thirsting, for yet another acrimonious sortie around Europe, and that there was a more overtly political reason for this than they had previously understood. What she could not bear to lose, they realised, was the populist appeal of the anti-EEC card. At a time when economic problems were piling up at home, the leader who was seen as struggling to the death against no fewer than eight foreign powers made much of her image of patriotic valour.

The Cabinet, however, did not agree. The decision to endorse the 30 May Brussels agreement was one of the quite rare instances during the Thatcher era when the Cabinet collectively gathered sufficient will to divert the prime minister from her favoured course. Hitherto, as sole negotiator at successive summits, she had sole right of decision on what to reject. On this occasion – and it irked her deeply – she was faced with something close to a *fait accompli* which she might overturn only at her peril.

H. Young, [76], pp. 189–90.

<h2>DOCUMENT 3   THATCHER: THE EC BUDGET AGREEMENT</h2>

Mrs Thatcher describes her reaction to the agreement. Unlike Document 2 she maintains that it was the merits of the agreement, rather than Cabinet pressure, that led her to accept it.

My immediate reaction was far from favourable. The deal involved a net budget contribution in 1980 far higher than envisaged at Luxembourg. It appeared from Peter's figures that we would pay rather less under the new package in 1981, though to some extent this was sleight of hand, reflecting different assumptions about the size of that year's total budget. But the Brussels proposal had one great advantage: it now offered us a three-year solution. We were promised a major review of the budget problem by mid-1981 and if this had not been achieved (as proved to be the case) the Commission would make proposals along the lines of the formula for 1980–81 and the Council would act accordingly. The other elements of the Brussels package relating to agriculture, lamb and fisheries, were more or less acceptable. We had to agree to a 5 per cent rise in farm prices. Overall, the deal marked a refund of two-thirds of our net contribution and it marked a huge progress from the position the Government had inherited. I therefore decided to accept the offer.

M. Thatcher, [28], p. 86.

DOCUMENT 4   A 'WET' CRITIQUE OF EARLY ECONOMIC
POLICY

This document comes from the memoirs of Jim Prior (Employment Secretary 1979-81; Northern Ireland Secretary 1981–84). Prior was an arch-wet and found Mrs Thatcher's economic policy quite unbelievable. In this document he analyses the thinking behind the first Budget and the entire economic strategy.

Margaret's economic policy was dictated by the belief that sound money was the essential requirement for a successful and stable nation. As far as she was concerned, inflation was a much greater social evil than unemployment, and in any case, in her eyes, you could only cure unemployment by controlling inflation. She thus felt free to castigate all post-war governments, Labour and Conservative, because she reckoned their policies had made our problems progressively worse.

The idea of pumping money into the economy to reduce unemployment was anathema. If only a better balance could be achieved between the public sector and the private, with less public spending, the economy would expand in response to market forces. It was a very simplistic approach, a combination of her own instincts founded in the corner shop at Grantham, laid over by a veneer from Hayek and Friedman. In a world increasingly interdependent and with a people used to a welfare state, it looked an unpromising scenario. It was on the basis of this kind of simple-minded analysis that Margaret and Geoffrey concocted the first Budget, which was to do so much harm. ...

... All through the early period of Margaret's Government I felt the Treasury team were out of their depth. They were all theorists – either barristers or, in the case of Nigel Lawson, a journalist. None of them had any experience of running a whelk stall, let alone a decent-sized company.

J. Prior, [25], pp. 119–22.

DOCUMENT 5   RULING OUT U-TURNS: PRIVATELY

By 1980, as the economic situation continued to deteriorate, many called for the government to change its economic policy. Sir John Hoskyns (Head of Thatcher's Policy Unit 1979-82) recalls Mrs Thatcher's reaction to the possibility of a U-turn.

In the middle of 1980 when unemployment was already rising fast, bankruptcies were rising, and it was obviously all getting pretty hairy, I and one or two other advisers went to her and asked, 'If there is ever going to be any sort of U-turn on policy you absolutely must think about it now. ... We wanted to be absolutely sure that if, in fact, privately there was a view in her mind – or in that of any of her colleagues – that there might have to be any significant change in policy, one really had to start preparing the ground for it, rather than be made to look utterly idiotic at the last minute. She simply said, 'You know, I would rather go down than do that, so forget it.' And I just remember saying, 'Thank you very much, because we now know exactly where we stand and I think you are absolutely right.' There was very impressive readiness to look right through to the end and say, 'That is what we'll do.'

H. Young and A. Sloman, [77], p. 65.

DOCUMENT 6   **RULING OUT U-TURNS: PUBLICLY**

By the 1980 party conference the worsening of many economic statistics, particularly the rise in unemployment, led many in the Conservative Party to question the government's economic strategy. Mrs Thatcher sought to reaffirm that, although she understood the pain caused by unemployment, she would not be deflected from her central aim of bringing down inflation.

Inflation destroys nations and societies as surely as invading armies do. Inflation is the parent of unemployment. It is the unseen robber of those who have saved.

No policy which puts at risk the defeat of inflation – however great its short-term attraction – can be right. ...

... Let me make it clear beyond doubt: I am profoundly concerned about unemployment. Human dignity and self-respect are undermined when men and women are condemned to idleness. The waste of a country's most precious resource, the talent and energy of its people, makes it the bounden duty of the Government to seek a real and lasting cure.

If I could press a button and genuinely solve the unemployment problem, do you think that I would not press that button this instant? ... This Government are pursuing the only policy which gives any hope of bringing our people back to real and lasting employment. ...

... To those waiting with bated breath for that favourite media catchphrase, the 'U turn', I have only one thing to say: 'You turn if you want to. The lady's not for turning.' I say that not only to you, but to our friends overseas and also to those who are not our friends.

M. Thatcher, [30], pp. 109–20.

DOCUMENT 7   GOW'S MEMORANDUM

On 27 February 1981, Ian Gow, Mrs Thatcher's Parliamentary Private Secretary, sent her a memorandum that reported a significant drop in backbench morale.

Prime Minister

1. I am sorry to say that there has been a noticeable deterioration in the morale of our backbenchers.
2. I attribute this to:–
   (a) Increasing concern about the extent of the recession and unemployment.
   (b) The perceived defeats for the Government on Coal and, to a lesser extent in the pay settlement for the water workers.
   (c) The size of the PSBR and the slowness with which interest rates are falling.
   (d) The insatiable appetite of the Public Sector – notably BL, BSC, NCB.
   (e) The Rate Support Grant.

M. Thatcher, [28], p. 132.

DOCUMENT 8   THE KEYNESIAN PETITION

With no real improvement in the economy in sight, in March 1981 364 leading academic economists published a statement criticising Mrs Thatcher's economic strategy and calling for a return to Keynesian policies. This document reproduces the statement from the front page of The Times *of 30 March.*

We who are all present or retired members of the economic staffs of British universities, are convinced that there is no basis in economic theory or supporting evidence for the Government's belief that by deflating demand they will bring inflation permanently under control and thereby induce an automatic recovery in output and employment; present policies will deepen the depression, erode the industrial base of our economy and threaten its social and political stability; there are alternative policies and the time has come to reject monetarist policies and consider urgently which alternative offers the best hope of sustained economic recovery.

The Times, [4], 30.3.81.

DOCUMENT 9   THE FALKLANDS EMERGENCY DEBATE

On 2 April 1982 Argentina invaded the Falkland Islands. The next day there was an emergency debate in the House of Commons. The mood was one of outrage at the invasion of British sovereign territory and Mrs Thatcher was able to harness this to secure support for government's stance. This document is from the speech she made in the emergency debate.

The House meets this Saturday to respond to a situation of great gravity. We are here because, for the first time for many years, British sovereign territory has been invaded by a foreign power. ... I must tell the House that the Falkland Islands and their dependencies remain British territory. No aggression and no invasion can alter that simple fact. It is the Government's objective to see that the islands are freed from occupation and are returned to British administration at the earliest possible moment. ...

... The people of the Falkland Islands, like the people of the United Kingdom, are an island race. Their way of life is British; their allegiance is to the Crown. They are few in number, but they have the right to live in peace, to choose their own way of life and to determine their own allegiance. It is the wish of the British people and the duty of Her Majesty's Government to do everything that we can to uphold that right. That will be our hope and our endeavour and, I believe, the resolve of every member of the House.

M. Thatcher, [30], pp. 149–57.

DOCUMENT 10   REJOICE!

After the retaking of South Georgia by British Forces on 25 April 1982 with no British casualties, Mrs Thatcher was determined to secure positive news coverage. In this document Mrs Thatcher claims that some interpreted her remarks differently from the way she intended, when she announced the news with John Nott on 26 April.

A remark of mine was misinterpreted, sometimes wilfully. After John Nott had made his statement journalists tried to ask questions. 'What happens next Mr Nott? Are we going to declare war on Argentina Mrs Thatcher?' It seemed as if they preferred to press us on these issues rather than to report news that would raise the nation's spirits and give the Falklanders new heart. I was irritated and intervened to stop them: 'just rejoice at that news and congratulate our forces and the marines ... Rejoice'. I meant that they should rejoice in the bloodless recapture of South Georgia, not in the war itself. To me war is not a matter for rejoicing. But some pretended otherwise.

M. Thatcher, [28], pp. 208–9.

DOCUMENT 11   THE FALKLANDS BATTLE GROUP
COMMANDER, SANDY WOODWARD,
EXPLAINS THE DECISION TO SINK THE
GENERAL BELGRANO

In this extract from Woodward's memoirs, he explains the military threat posed by the General Belgrano *and the decision to sink it using the submarine* HMS Conqueror. *Despite later allegations of a political motive behind Mrs Thatcher's decision to change the rules of engagement to allow the* General Belgrano *to be sunk, Woodward's account strongly supports the view that this decision was taken purely on military grounds.*

... it all looked to me like a classic pincer movement attack on the British Battle Group. To take the worst possible case, *Belgrano* and her escorts could now set off towards us and, steaming through the dark, launch an Exocet attack on us from one direction just as we were preparing to receive a missile and bomb strike from the other. ... There was but one fast solution. I had to take out the one claw of the pincer ... the *Belgrano* and her destroyers ...

... After quick but careful consideration of the military advice, the Prime Minister and the War Cabinet authorised changes to the ROE [Rules of Engagement] which would permit *Conqueror* to attack the *Belgrano* group ...

... We now know that at 0810 *Belgrano* and her escorts reversed course, and were in fact on their way home. But they headed back to the west on a gentle zig-zag, not apparently in any great hurry or with any obvious purpose. When I became aware of their westerly course that afternoon, I still had no reliable evidence as to their intentions. For all I knew they might have received a signal telling them to return to base; but perhaps they had only been told to wait and come back tonight; perhaps they hadn't been told anything ...

... It was not until 2245 that we received a signal from Northwood [UK HQ] to tell us that *HMS Conqueror* had sunk the *General Belgrano*. ... What no one knew then was that [we] ... had sent the navy of Argentina home for good.

S. Woodward, [33], pp. 147–64.

DOCUMENT 12   THE CENTRAL POLICY REVIEW STAFF
PROPOSALS OF 1982

This document concerns a CPRS paper whose radical suggestions caused the
government much embarrassment when it was leaked to The Economist. *This*
document comes from the article in The Economist *that carried the first*
details of the leaked paper.

The think-tank's paper was circulated along with other Cabinet papers on
September 7th. It came with the seal of approval of the Treasury, which rec-
ommended that it form the basis of a six-month study of a public spending
strategy for the rest of the decade. This means that its ideas were not pulled
out of the ether and that it has more significance than most other think-tank
papers. Here are details of its contents ...
... Education. Its most controversial suggestion is to end state funding for
all institutions of higher education. Instead, fees would be set at market rates.
... The paper also says that there would be great savings if the state no longer
had to provide for primary and secondary school education, but it acknowledges the political difficulties of abolishing state schooling ...
... Social Security. Big savings can be made, says the paper, if all social
security payments – from pensions to supplementary benefits – no longer rise
in line with inflation ...
... Health. The paper suggests replacing the National Health Service with
private health insurance ... the less well-off might underinsure, so the paper
suggests that there might have to be a compulsory minimum of private insurance for everyone. In the meantime savings could be made by charging for
visits to the doctor and more for drugs ...
... Mrs Thatcher sympathises with the think-tank's drift. But she is now in
no doubt that to pursue such a radical course risks splitting her party wide
open.

The Economist, [9], 18.9.82.

DOCUMENT 13   THE ROLE OF MONETARISM IN THE 1983
ELECTION VICTORY

In this document, Peter Jenkins ponders the 1983 victory and considers the
role of monetarism. Although he regards it as an economic failure, he suggests
that the economic strategy may have had a deeper effect on the attitudes of
the electorate.

Whatever its economic consequences, the 1981 Budget was for Mrs Thatcher
the triumph of her will. She had defied the conventional wisdom. There were
riots in the cities that summer to add further to the alarm of those who

believed that she was pressing beyond the limits of social and political tolerance. That autumn, as we have seen, she broke all records of unpopularity. Odds were being laid against her survival in office ... eighteen months later, she was to sweep back into office in defiance of the three million unemployed. The war to recover the Falklands had intervened and the 'Falklands Factor' contributed to the remarkable victory of 1983. So did the 1981 schism on the Left and the 'Foot Factor'. Yet these are insufficient explanations for the 1983 triumph and obscure its meaning. For in the meanwhile something more extraordinary had happened: the country had lowered its expectations and consented once more to be governed.

The success of the government in this respect is not to be measured by the achievement, or non-achievement, of arcane money targets. It is more likely that inflation was brought down in spite of monetarism than because of it, chiefly by general deflation and falling commodity prices ...

... for the public, monetarism, whatever it was, became synonymous with Thatcherism. Moreover, it symbolised a break with the past. By 1983 many were ready to blame unemployment on the international situation, not on the government of the day. Moreover, they were ready to blame it on the prodigalities of the past, on prolix over-manning, on trade union militancy and bloody-mindedness. Their daily experience told people that a great deal of what Margaret Thatcher was saying was true. Blaming unemployment on external factors, or on forces beyond the government's control, was a stage in the process of blaming unemployment on nobody. The appeal of market economics lies in precisely this: it is a means of avoiding social responsibility. There is no economic logic, no logic of any kind, in saying that because Keynesianism no longer achieves its purpose, the 'laws of the market', whose deficiencies Keynes had addressed, have miraculously been restored. 'Thatcherism' was a way of filling an intellectual and a moral vacuum.

P. Jenkins, [52], pp. 153–4.

DOCUMENT 14   THATCHER'S REACTION TO THE
                INVASION OF GRENADA

On 25 October 1983, US Forces invaded Grenada as a response to a coup that had allowed extreme Marxists to seize power. However, although Grenada was part of the Commonwealth, Reagan only consulted Mrs Thatcher when it was too late to stop the invasion. While publicly she was reluctant to condemn Reagan, in this document her daughter, Carol, reveals that her private reaction was far less restrained.

She was dismayed and felt utterly let down, but most of all angry. It placed her in the embarrassing position of having to explain how a member of the Commonwealth had been invaded by our closest ally.

Denis heard one half of the telephone call. 'She didn't half tick him [Reagan] off on the telephone. "You have invaded the Queen's territory and you didn't even say a word to me," she said to him, very upset. I think that Reagan was a bit shocked. There was nothing gentle about her tone – and not much diplomacy either. He got a prime ticking off. I think his reasons were good enough, but to invade British territory without a by your leave or without any notice was wrong.'

C. Thatcher, [74], p. 210.

DOCUMENT 15   **THE SINGLE EUROPEAN ACT**

This document comes from the act that was agreed at the Luxembourg EC Council in December 1985 and formally signed on 17 February 1986. The chief attraction for Mrs Thatcher was the removal of surviving barriers to a single market for goods and services throughout the Community, but this document illustrates that the Single European Act also provided for the further European integration that Mrs Thatcher was soon to proclaim herself determined to avoid.

... The Community shall adopt measures with the aim of progressively establishing the internal market over a period expiring on 31 December 1992. ... The internal market shall comprise an area without internal frontiers in which the free movement of goods, persons, services and capital is ensured in accordance with the provisions of this Treaty ...
... Co-operation in Economic and Monetary policy
(Economic and Monetary Union)
In order to ensure the convergence of economic and monetary policies which is necessary for the further development of the Community, Member States ... shall take account of the experience acquired in co-operating within the framework of the European Monetary System (EMS) and in developing the ECU ...
... Social Policy ...
... acting by a qualified majority on a proposal from the Commission, in co-operation with the European Parliament and after consulting the Economic and Social Committee, shall adopt, by means of directives, minimum requirements for gradual implementation, having regard to the conditions and technical rules obtaining in each of the Member States.

The Single European Act, HMSO (Cmd 372).

DOCUMENT 16   THATCHER'S ROLE IN THE GCHQ UNION
               BAN

On 25 January 1984, Sir Geoffrey Howe announced a ban on trade unions at
Government Communications Headquarters (GCHQ). This document comes
from Howe's memoirs, where he admits that failing to consult trade union
leaders led to much of the ensuing hostility, but also suggests that Mrs
Thatcher, herself, must take much of the blame for the adverse consequences
of the decision.

Granted that we all had to share responsibility for the non-consultative
secrecy with which we had shaped and conducted this policy – and not one of
us, it must be said, had challenged that – could we not have done more to save
the government from such a disastrous demonstration of unyielding hostility to
trade unionism in all its forms? Well, we could certainly, and in our private
discussions we did try. Tom King, Robert Armstrong and I did all canvass
with Margaret the one solution that could have secured an acceptable outcome: the so-called 'card in the pocket' solution. This involved exactly the
same basic prescription, with the exception that a trade unionist would have
been entitled to retain his union membership, and only that. There would and
should have been no union organization at or connected with GCHQ, but the
basic right of membership would have been preserved ...
    ... It could well have worked. At least it deserved a try. But not for Marga-
ret. This was a case where she was at the end driven by her 'all or nothing'
absolutist instinct. She could not find room in her thinking for acceptance of
the parallel legitimacy of someone else's loyalty. It was probably the clearest
example I had seen so far of one of Margaret's most tragic failings: an inability to appreciate, still less accommodate, somebody else's patriotism ...
    ... A citizen, she seemed to feel, could never safely be allowed to carry
more than one card in his or her pocket, and at GCHQ that could only be
Her Majesty's card.

G. Howe, [21], pp. 347–8.

DOCUMENT 17   ARTHUR SCARGILL RAISES THE MINERS'
               SPIRITS

This document comes from Scargill's presidential address to the extraordinary
annual conference of the NUM. Throughout the strike Scargill used his
speeches to try to strengthen the miners by predicting that the NUM would
win. This document is an example of such a morale boosting speech.

Through the police, the judiciary, the social security system – whichever way
seems possible – the full weight of the state is being brought to bear upon us

in an attempt to try and break this strike. ... On the picket lines, riot police in full battle gear, on horseback and on foot, accompanied by police dogs, have been unleashed in violent attacks upon our members ...

Throughout this dispute ... it has been clear that the Board's negotiators are manipulated in every move by the Prime Minister, who seems obsessed with trying to defeat the National Union of Mineworkers ...

... There can be no compromise in our union's principled opposition to the Coal Board's pit closure programme. Ours is a supremely noble aim: to defend pits, jobs, communities and the right to work. We are now entering a crucial phase in our battle for the survival of this industry. For the first time since the strike began, even the pundits and the experts have started to admit that the pendulum is swinging in favour of the NUM ...

... The sacrifices and the hardships have forged a unique commitment among our members. They will ensure that the NUM wins this most crucial battle in the history of our industry. Comrades, I salute you for your magnificent achievements and for your support – together, we cannot fail.

The Times, [4], 12.7.84.

DOCUMENT 18   ANGLO-IRISH AGREEMENT: JOINT COMMUNIQUÉ

This document is an extract from the communiqué issued by the British and Irish leaders on 15 November 1985. It was the idea of the Irish government having a consultative role in governing Northern Ireland that was to provoke Unionist indignation.

The Prime Minister and the Taoiseach signed a formal and binding agreement between their two Governments, which will enter into force as soon as each Government has notified the other of acceptance. The Agreement has the aims of promoting peace and stability in Northern Ireland; helping to reconcile the two major traditions in Ireland; creating a new climate of friendship and co-operation between the people of the two countries; and improving co-operation in combating terrorism.

The Agreement deals in particular with the status of Northern Ireland and the establishment of an Inter-governmental Conference in which the Irish Government will put forward views about proposals concerning stated aspects of Northern Ireland affairs; in which the promotion of cross-border co-operation will be discussed; and in which determined efforts will be made to resolve any differences between the two Governments ...

The Times, [4], 16.11.85.

The next four documents all concern the Westland Affair of early 1986.

DOCUMENT 19   **INGHAM AND THE LEAKED LETTER**

One of the potentially most damaging incidents for Mrs Thatcher during the Westland Affair was the leaking of a confidential law officer's letter which damaged Heseltine's case. For many years the question of who actually authorised the DTI Press Officer, Colette Bowe, to release selected passages of the letter remained highly controversial. In this document the much accused Bernard Ingham, Mrs Thatcher's Chief Press Secretary, pleads not guilty.

... my eyebrows shot up – [Bowe] told me that she had been given Ministerial permission to 'leak' the Solicitor-General's letter to Mr Heseltine claiming that there were 'material inaccuracies' in Mr Heseltine's letter ... Leaving aside Ministerial approval, I expressed grave reservations about the plan to give this information to Chris Moncrieff (PA) and wondered whether the point could not be made public in another way. I was told that the news needed to be in the public domain before a Westland press conference at 4 pm. And Colette Bowe made it clear to me that the DTI hoped that Number 10 – namely myself – would do the leaking. I refused to do so point blank. I had no authority to disclose the Solicitor-General's letter. I told Colette Bowe that I had to keep the Prime Minister above that sort of thing. At no time was I asked to approve of the disclosure. I could not have done so without seeking Mrs Thatcher's specific permission, and I would not have been prepared to put such an idea to her.

What I ought to have done – and regret to this day that I did not – was advise Colette Bowe, regardless of her Minister's permission, to have nothing to do with the ploy herself. It is on the basis of this failure that the DTI felt able to claim that I – and, indeed, Charles Powell – had accepted that the letter should be disclosed. It was at best tacit acceptance in the sense that I did not actively object to a Ministerial decision to disclose it. Looking back on the entire incident, I can only put my failure to do so down to the extraordinary circumstances created by the breakdown of collective Cabinet responsibility.

B. Ingham, [22], p. 335.

DOCUMENT 20   **MICHAEL CRICK'S VERDICT ON THE LEAK**

This document is an extract from Crick's biography of Michael Heseltine. Crick's verdict on the leaked letter differs considerably from the primary evidence of Document 19.

To leak the advice of a law officer, without his knowledge or blessing, was a far more serious offence than even the wide-scale disclosures of the previous

few weeks. Mayhew's letter had been marked 'Confidential', the same classifi-
cation as the material Clive Ponting sent to Tam Dalyell. Leon Brittan would
soon admit that he had authorized Colette Bowe's leak, and years later he
revealed that he had received 'express approval from Number Ten' – from
Thatcher's two most senior advisers, Bernard Ingham and Charles Powell. (As
befits a QC who once specialized in libel, Brittan is very precise in what he
says; his use of the word 'express' refuted the official explanation at the time
that he had misunderstood Downing Street's wishes.)

Number Ten and the DTI later produced spurious arguments about the
need to get Mayhew's letter into the public domain before a Westland press
conference that afternoon. In the event, Heseltine was able to supply Mayhew
with extra papers to back his case and which seemed to satisfy the Solicitor-
General, though this fact was largely ignored amid all the fuss. The true purpose of the leak was obvious: to damage Michael Heseltine. The *Sun* took the
bait, emblazoning the words 'YOU LIAR!' down its front page. It later apolo-
gized and made a gift to charity in lieu of damages.

M. Crick, [42], pp. 284–5.

DOCUMENT 21   **THATCHER DEFENDS HERSELF**

*As the tension over the leaked letter and the entire Westland Affair mounted,
Thatcher attempted to extricate herself and her staff from any blame in a
speech to the House of Commons on 23 January. This document provides
Hugo Young's account of that speech, which should be compared with the
account in Document 22.*

The negotiated statement was duly made. The prime minister delivered most
of it in a low, fast blur. She presented herself as not only innocent but almost
completely ignorant. 'An enormous number of facts were not known to me
until yesterday when I received the results of the inquiry,' she said. She admitted that her own officials had been involved, but found words to exculpate
both them and herself. On the one hand, she would have instructed, had she
been consulted, that 'a different way must be found of making the relevant
facts known'. On the other hand, insofar as her officials thought they were
speaking for her when they told the DTI that the contents of the Mayhew letter should be put into the public domain, 'they were right.' As for the reason
why the whole unfortunate affair had occurred, this was entirely comprehen-
sible. It was to do, she said, with the overriding demands of commercial reality. A business decision was at stake. Westland were holding a press
conference at four o'clock. They absolutely had to know what the legal opinion of Heseltine's view was. It was probably the most unconvincing statement
she ever made to the House of Commons.

H. Young, [76], p. 452.

DOCUMENT 22   A DIARIST'S VIEW OF THATCHER'S
PERFORMANCE

This document is an extract from Alan Clark's diary. Clark was a Conservative MP whose admiration for Thatcher knew no bounds and in this document he records being shown Thatcher's speech for the debate of 23 January. He also records the Commons reception that this speech and another speech on the matter, that Thatcher had to give on 27 January, received.

Friday, 24 January
Then, unexpectedly, the Chief Whip [John Wakeham] came over and sat with us. He showed me a copy of the statement. I read a few paragraphs, started a *faux-rire.* I couldn't help it. 'I'm sorry, John. I simply can't keep a straight face.' The paper passed from hand to hand. Others agreed, but were too polite to say so.
How *can* she say these things without faltering?
But she did. Kept her nerve beautifully.
I was sitting close by, and could see her riffling her notes, and turning the pages of the speech. Her hand did not shake *at all.* It was almost as if the House, half horrified, half dumb with admiration, was cowed. ... Serene and haughty, at its end she swept from the Chamber, and a little later came to a meeting of the '22. The mood was wholly supportive of her, and the Scapegoat was duly tarred.

House of Commons – Monday, 27 January
Every seat in the House had been booked with a prayer card, and they were all up the gangways.
    For a few seconds Kinnock had her cornered, and you could see fear in those blue eyes. But then he had an attack of wind, gave her time to recover. A brilliant performance. Shameless and brave. We are out of the wood.

A. Clark, [13], pp. 133–5.

DOCUMENT 23   HOWE AND THATCHER

This document is a cartoon which appeared in the Australian press in August 1986, a copy of which was presented to Howe by the Australian Prime Minister Bob Hawke. At the time it appeared Mrs Thatcher was pursuing a very tough line against imposing sanctions on South Africa in protest at apartheid, a line that Howe would have liked to relax. As the Howe–Thatcher relationship progessed, this cartoon became only more appropriate.

G. Howe, [21], on plates between pp. 592 and 593.

DOCUMENT 24   LAWSON ATTACKS THE POLL TAX

A Specification Report on the potential poll tax was produced in March 1985. Mrs Thatcher strongly supported it, but Lawson was fiercely opposed. This document comes from a memorandum of 16 May 1985 in which Lawson set out his viewpoint, and provides a sharp contrast to Document 25.

I agree that our system of local government finance cannot be left as it is, and that radical change is needed ...

   ... It is only when we come to the question of what local tax we should have that I have to depart altogether from the proposals in the Specification

Report. The report recognizes that a flat-rate poll tax would be politically unsustainable; even with a rebate scheme the package would have 'an unacceptable impact' on certain types of household.

The biggest gainers would be better off households in high rateable value properties; the losers would be poorer households, particularly larger ones. ... A pensioner couple in Inner London could find themselves paying 22 per cent of their net income in poll tax, whereas a better off couple in the suburbs would pay only 1 per cent.

... Whatever system we adopt, we should learn from this year's experiences in Scotland: we should always ensure that revaluations – and other changes – are phased in over a reasonable period. The problems of an old-style revaluation upheaval would, of course, be magnified many times during the period of transition from rates to poll tax. This is not simply a hideous political problem: local authorities would seize the opportunity to bump up their spending and revenue and blame it all on the imposition by the Government of an alien system of taxation. ... The proposal for a poll tax would be completely unworkable and politically catastrophic. A radical reform of the rating system seems a more attractive option.

N. Lawson, [23], pp. 573–4.

DOCUMENT 25   **THATCHER DEFENDS THE POLL TAX**

The decision to replace the domestic rates with the Community Charge (aka poll tax) was probably the most unpopular decision Thatcher made and played an important part in her downfall. The poll tax was later abandoned under John Major but Thatcher still believes she was right to introduce the tax, as this extract from her memoirs shows.

The charge became a rallying point for those who opposed me, both within the Conservative Party and on the far left. Had I not been facing problems on other fronts – above all, had the Cabinet and Party held their nerve – I could have ridden through the difficulties. Indeed, the community charge, having been modified in many ways, was beginning to work at the very time it was abandoned. Given time, it would have been seen as one of the most far-reaching and beneficial reforms ever made in the working of local government. Above all, the community charge offered a last chance of responsible, efficient, local democracy in Britain. Its abandonment will mean that more and more powers will pass to central government, that upward pressures on public spending and taxation will increase accordingly, and that still fewer people of ability will become local councillors.

M. Thatcher, [28], p. 642.

DOCUMENT 26   A PUBLIC RIFT OVER EXCHANGE RATE
POLICY EMERGES

This document comes from a report in The Sunday Times. *The report high-lighted conflicting replies that Lawson and Mrs Thatcher had given in the Commons earlier in the week over the government's exchange rate policy. This began the harmful, although accurate, speculation of a rift between the Prime Minister and her Chancellor over this issue.*

Nigel Lawson's future as Chancellor of the Exchequer was the subject of much speculation yesterday after Mrs Thatcher's decision, supported by the Bank of England, to abandon his exchange rate policy, the keystone of his economic strategy for the past year ...

... Thatcher told Lawson that she was determined to keep the inflation rate down, even at the cost of high interest rates and a rising pound and Leigh-Pemberton backed her to the hilt. ... In the end Lawson reluctantly agreed to let the pound float as a short-term tactical measure. Thatcher, however, had a more substantial change of policy in mind.

On Tuesday she told Neil Kinnock, the Labour leader, that she planned no reduction in interest rates. She said the only way to deal with the pound's rise was 'either to have excessive intervention which would lead to inflation, or to deal with the matter by interest rates, which would not be in the interests of inflation'.

This conflicted with the previous day's message from the Treasury that the government remained committed to exchange stability, that it wanted to preserve the competitiveness of industry and that if the pound rose too far, a cut in interest rates was not ruled out.

The differences between Thatcher and Lawson were on display in the Commons again on Thursday. Lawson tried to talk the pound down with a statement that 'any further significant rise in the exchange rate, certainly against the deutschmark, would in my opinion be unlikely to be sustainable'. But Thatcher, who entered the Commons a few minutes later, said that so far as the pound was concerned, there was 'no way you can buck the market'.

The Sunday Times, [8], 13.3.88.

DOCUMENT 27   **HEALING THE RIFT**

The division over exchange rate policy was laid bare on 12 May, when Mrs Thatcher refused to say that she agreed with her Chancellor. This was very damaging for the government and therefore Lawson and Mrs Thatcher agreed a statement for Prime Minister's Questions on 17 May to end the rift. This document contains that statement, given in reply to a question about exchange rate policy from Neil Kinnock, and Lawson's assessment of its success in healing the rift.

I am sure that he [Kinnock] would like a detailed reply. My right hon. Friend and I entirely agree [*interruption*] that we must maintain a firm monetary policy and a downward pull on inflation. I agree completely with my right hon. Friend's Budget speech, every bit of it, which is more than the right hon. Gentleman the Leader of the Opposition does.

The right hon. Gentleman asked about exchange rate policy. It is a part of overall economic policy. As I indicated a moment ago, he will note that we have taken interest rates down three times in the last two months. That was clearly intended to affect the exchange rate. We use the available levers, both interest rates and intervention, as seems right in the circumstances, and [*interruption*] it would be a great mistake to think at any time that sterling was a one-way bet.

Our back-benchers were delighted by what seemed an unequivocal endorsement of my policy and the end of the rift between Margaret and myself. William Clark, the long-serving Chairman of the back-bench Finance Committee, who had been among those most concerned by the rift, asked her 'Does not today's reduction [in interest rates] prove beyond peradventure that there is complete and utter unanimity in the management of our economy under the capable management of the Chancellor?' Margaret replied with the single word 'Yes'.

N. Lawson, [23], pp. 837–8.

DOCUMENT 28   **THE BRUGES WATERSHED**

This document comes from the speech Mrs Thatcher delivered to the College of Europe, Bruges on 20 September 1988. At a time when many in Europe, and some in the Conservative Party, were pushing for greater European integration, Mrs Thatcher set out her alternative vision. The speech was condemned throughout Europe and helped to polarise opposition to her leadership in the Conservative Party.

... Over the centuries we have fought to prevent Europe from falling under the dominance of a single power. We have fought and we have died for her freedom. Only miles from here in Belgium lie the bodies of 120,000 British soldiers who died in the First World War. Had it not been for that willingness to fight and to die, Europe would have been united long before now – but not in liberty, not in justice ...

... And let me be quite clear: Britain does not dream of some cosy, isolated existence on the fringes of the European Community. Our destiny is in Europe, as part of the Community ...

... My first guiding principle is this: willing and active co-operation between independent sovereign states is the best way to build a successful European Community. To try to suppress nationhood and concentrate power at the centre of a European conglomerate would be highly damaging and would jeopardize the objectives we seek to achieve. Europe will be stronger precisely because it has France as France, Spain as Spain, Britain as Britain, each with its own customs, traditions and identity. It would be folly to try to fit them into some sort of identikit European personality ...

... working more closely together does *not* require power to be centralized in Brussels or decisions to be taken by an appointed bureaucracy. ... We have not successfully rolled back the frontiers of the state in Britain only to see them re-imposed at a European level, with a European super-state exercising a new dominance from Brussels.

Certainly we want to see Europe more united and with a greater sense of common purpose. But it must be in a way which preserves the different traditions, Parliamentary powers and sense of national pride in one's own country; for these have been the source of Europe's vitality through the centuries.

M. Thatcher, [30], pp. 315–25.

The next three documents all refer to what passed between Howe, Lawson and Mrs Thatcher before the Madrid European Council of 26 June 1989. Through memos and meetings, Howe and Lawson sought to persuade Thatcher to adopt a more positive negotiating position which could include a non-legally binding pledge to join the ERM by the end of 1992. At a final meeting they threatened to resign if she did not take their advice. The disagreement between the three participants is over the motive for Howe and Lawson's action and whether or not they succeeded in forcing Mrs Thatcher to handle the Madrid Council as they wished.

DOCUMENT 29   THE AMBUSH BEFORE MADRID: THATCHER

In this document Mrs Thatcher explains why she believed Lawson and Howe acted as they did but triumphantly explains that by failing to set a date for ERM entry she successfully called their bluff.

On Wednesday 14 June 1980, just twelve days before the European Council in Madrid, Geoffrey Howe and Nigel Lawson mounted an ambush ...

... I knew that Geoffrey had put Nigel up to this. He had been in a great state about the European election campaign which had not gone well for us. I knew that he had always thought that he might one day become Leader of the Conservative Party and Prime Minister – an ambition which became more passionate as it was slipping away from him. He considered himself – with some justice – as an important contributor to our past successes. This quiet, gentle, but deeply ambitious man – with whom my relations had become progressively worse as my exasperation at his insatiable appetite for compromise led me sometimes to lash out at him in front of others – was now out to make trouble for me if he possibly could. Above all, I suspect, he thought that he had become indispensable – a dangerous illusion for a politician. There is no other explanation for what he now did and put Nigel up to doing.

* * *

Back home, Cabinet began as usual at 10.30 on Thursday 29 June. Normally, I would sit at my place with my back to the door as Cabinet ministers trooped in. This time, however, I stood in the doorway – waiting. But there were no resignations. The condition that there must be a date for our joining the ERM might never have been mentioned. Nigel Lawson even managed the remark that Madrid had gone rather well, hadn't it. He certainly had a nerve, I thought: but then Nigel always did. That was one of his engaging characteristics.

M. Thatcher, [28], pp. 710–13.

DOCUMENT 30   **THE AMBUSH BEFORE MADRID: HOWE**

In this document, Howe suggests a different motive for his actions from that expressed in Document 29. In sharp contrast to Document 29 he claims that after the encounter before Madrid the view shared by him and Lawson prevailed. This is because, although she did not set a date, Thatcher shifted her negotiating position very much in the way they had suggested.

There had been no ulterior motive to our manoeuvres, no personalized conspiracy. Nor would there be. We were engaged in a joint exercise, jointly conceived – and with a single legitimate purpose. We both felt strongly the need to influence for the better Margaret's handling of Madrid, and specifically to do so by a clear tautening of the 'time is ripe' formula. We had agreed that, if this case was to make any headway at Number 10, it needed joint presentation (how right we were!). And we had agreed to back our view with a seriously intended statement of our willingness to resign, if the case was brushed aside. We had done just that. Nigel was now to stay in London and I to go with Margaret to Madrid. We each had next to see what happened there.

* * *

The whole occasion [Madrid] was perceived as a victory for the United Kingdom, and two days later presented and received as such by Margaret Thatcher to the House of Commons. It was as close to the outcome for which Nigel and I had been pressing as we might have hoped ...
... The only ambiguity was about the way in which Margaret Thatcher viewed the event. For in her memoirs she gives gleeful prominence to the way in which, for the following Thursday's Cabinet (29 June), she 'stood in the

doorway – waiting. But there were no resignations.' Nigel and I had thus, in her eyes, acknowledged her 'victory'. For, whatever else she had conceded, she had avoided setting a precise date for sterling's entry into the ERM. I have to say that the significance of this piece of retrospective theatre, if such it was, was completely lost on both the other actors in the drama: neither of us had noticed or have since been able to recall any change in Margaret's routine. Certainly we were both satisfied that the synergy of our earlier confrontation with the Prime Minister had produced a result that was good for Britain, and one with which all three of us could be content. So, for a time, it seemed.

G. Howe, [21], pp. 580–4.

DOCUMENT 31   THE AMBUSH BEFORE MADRID: LAWSON

In this document the final player in the drama, Nigel Lawson, explains why he acted as he did. As might be expected, this document bears a far greater resemblance to Document 30 than 29.

Geoffrey explained that he was deeply concerned that Margaret would badly mishandle the Madrid European Council which was now less than a fortnight off. Her manner at these meetings had become increasingly strident and confrontational, something that was no longer bringing any useful results; and the issues at stake were, thanks to EMU, more important than ever. I replied that, while I did not go along with everything in the minute, I agreed with him about the dangers we faced at Madrid, the risk of Margaret mishandling the Council, and the desirability of underlining the genuineness of our commitment to join the ERM by giving a latest date by which we would enter the mechanism.

* * *

Margaret clearly felt that she had stood her ground. She had refused to give a deadline for ERM entry, and had produced a new formula which, although very different from the old one, would, she believed, give her almost as much freedom to decide that the time for entry had not yet come ... But despite all Ingham's efforts to sell the new formula as only a minor change, the press, perhaps influenced in part by her new tone of voice, universally interpreted it as a major new development and a big step towards ERM membership. And a particular interpretation of the Madrid conditions did indeed assist my successor, John Major, to persuade a Margaret Thatcher weakened by my resignation to assent to ERM membership some 16 months later.

N. Lawson, [23], pp. 930–4.

DOCUMENT 32   **THE DEPUTY PRIME MINISTER**

*One of the key elements in persuading Howe to accept what would otherwise
have been clear demotion was the title of Deputy Prime Minister. However,
this document, from Howe's memoirs, suggests that the poor state of the
Howe/Thatcher relationship would make it difficult for Howe to secure the
influence that Whitelaw, the last Deputy Prime Minister, enjoyed.*

If I was to stay on as Deputy Prime Minister, I said, then that would have to
be made clear – not just in formal terms but to the extent that I should be
assuming the role previously occupied by Willie Whitelaw. There was no
problem about the actual positions that I should hold. But the rest, said Margaret sensibly enough, would depend on how far we were able to recreate
confidence in each other. For Willie had been 'a very special kind of person'.
'That confidence', I replied, 'has been greatly damaged by today's events.'
Margaret demurred and said the problem was mutual ...

   The whole conversation, as we should both perhaps have seen more
clearly at the time, was scarcely an encouraging foundation for renewed partnership.

G.Howe, [21], p.590

DOCUMENT 33   **THE WALTERS DIVIDE**

*Although still in the USA, by 1988 Alan Walters was publishing articles in the
British press attacking Nigel Lawson's policies. However, in spite of this, on*

17 July 1988 it was announced that he would be returning as Thatcher's personal economic advisor. This document is a cartoon that appeared a few days later.

N. Lawson, [23], on plates between pp. 768 and 769.

DOCUMENT 34   NIGEL LAWSON'S RESIGNATION LETTER

Lawson resigned on 26 October 1989. This document is the text of his letter of resignation that he sent to Mrs Thatcher together with her reply.

Dear Margaret,

The successful conduct of economic policy is possible only if there is, *and is seen to be*, full agreement between the Prime Minister and the Chancellor of the Exchequer.

Recent events have confirmed that this essential requirement cannot be satisfied so long as Alan Walters remains your personal economic adviser.

I have therefore regretfully concluded that it is in the best interests of the Government for me to resign my office without further ado. ... I shall, of course, continue to support the Government from the back-benches.

Yours ever

Nigel

Dear Nigel,

It is with the most profound regret that I received your letter. We have spoken since and, as you know, it was my most earnest hope that you would continue your outstanding stewardship as Chancellor of the Exchequer at least for the rest of this Parliament. There is no difference in our basic economic beliefs, and Britain's economy is vastly stronger as a result of the policies which you and I and the Government have planned and pursued together...

... You have been responsible for possibly the most far-reaching reform of our tax structure this century, as well as for a period of unprecedented growth and prosperity. It is a matter of particular regret that you should decide to leave before your task is complete.

I know you will continue to support the Government vigorously from the back benches, but all in Cabinet will miss the great ability and breadth of understanding which you have brought to our deliberations.

Please thank Therese for her splendid support.

Yours ever

Margaret

N. Lawson, [23], pp. 964–5.

DOCUMENT 35 **RIDLEY SEALS HIS FATE**

Nicholas Ridley was a staunch Thatcher loyalist and had been in the Cabinet since 1983. His resignation on 14 July 1990 came as a result of his remarks about Germany and Europe in an interview in The Spectator. *This document reproduces some of the interview that was to deprive Mrs Thatcher of her last true Cabinet friend.*

It had seemed a topical way to engage his thoughts, since the day after we met, Herr Klaus-Otto Pohl, the president of the Bundesbank was visiting England to preach the joys of a joint European monetary policy.

'This is all a German racket designed to take over the whole of Europe. It has to be thwarted. This rushed take-over by the Germans on the worst possible basis, with the French behaving like poodles to the Germans, is absolutely intolerable'...

... Mr Ridley turned his fire – he was, as usual smoking heavily – onto the organisation as a whole.

'When I look at the institutions to which it is proposed that sovereignty is to be handed over, I'm aghast. Seventeen unelected reject politicians' – that includes you, Sir Leon – 'with no accountability to anybody, who are not responsible for raising taxes, just spending money, who are pandered to by a supine parliament which also is not responsible for raising taxes, already behaving with an arrogance I find breathtaking – the idea that one says, "OK, we'll give this lot our sovereignty," is unacceptable to me. I'm not against giving up sovereignty in principle, but not to this lot. You might just as well give it to Adolf Hitler, frankly' ...

... The point is, Mr Ridley's confidence in expressing his views on the German threat must owe a little something to the knowledge that they are not significantly different from those of the Prime Minister, who originally opposed German reunification, even though in public she is required not to be so indelicate as to draw comparisons between Herren Kohl and Hitler.

The Spectator, [11], 14.7.90.

DOCUMENT 36 **ET TU, BRUTE?**

This document comes from the resignation speech made by Sir Geoffrey Howe in the House of Commons on 13 November 1990. Howe was infuriated by Mrs Thatcher continually undermining any attempt by the government to adopt a positive attitude towards Europe, most recently by her public condemnation of John Major's hard ECU proposal. But this episode was just the final straw in his relationship with Mrs Thatcher, which, by now, had become impossible. It was a very powerful and bitter speech and turned out to be the point of no return for her premiership. Many interpreted the ending as a call to Heseltine to challenge for the leadership.

It has been suggested – even, indeed, by some of my right hon. and hon.

Friends – that I decided to resign solely because of questions of style and not on matters of substance at all. Indeed, if some of my former colleagues are to be believed, I must be the first Minister in history who has resigned because he was in full agreement with Government policy. The truth is that, in many aspects of politics, style and substance complement each other. Very often, they are two sides of the same coin ...

... It was remarkable – indeed, it was tragic – to hear my right hon. Friend dismissing, with such personalised incredulity, the very idea that the hard ECU proposal might find growing favour among the peoples of Europe, just as it was extraordinary to hear her assert that the whole idea of EMU might be open for consideration only by future generations. Those future generations are with us today.

How on earth are the Chancellor and the Governor of the Bank of England, commending the hard ECU as they strive to, to be taken as serious participants in the debate against that kind of background noise? ... It is rather like sending your opening batsmen to the crease only for them to find, the moment the first balls are bowled, that their bats have been broken before the game by the team captain ...

... In my letter of resignation, which I tendered with the utmost sadness and dismay, I said: "Cabinet Government is all about trying to persuade one another from within". That was my commitment to Government by persuasion – persuading colleagues and the nation. I have tried to do that as Foreign Secretary and since, but I realise now that the task has become futile: trying to stretch the meaning of words beyond what was credible, and trying to pretend that there was a common policy when every step forward risked being subverted by some casual comment or impulsive answer.

The conflict of loyalty, of loyalty to my right hon. Friend the Prime Minister – and, after all, in two decades together that instinct of loyalty is still very real – and of loyalty to what I perceive to be the true interests of the nation, has become all too great. I no longer believe it possible to resolve that conflict from within this Government. That is why I have resigned. In doing so, I have done what I believe to be right for my party and my country. The time has come for others to consider their own response to the tragic conflict of loyalties with which I have myself wrestled for perhaps too long.

G. Howe, [21], pp. 697–704.

CHRONOLOGY

1979

28 March	Callaghan's Labour government defeated in Commons no confidence vote. General election called.
30 March	Airey Neave murdered by bomb planted by INLA, a breakaway faction of the IRA.
3 May	Thatcher wins general election. Conservative majority: 43.
12 June	Howe delivers first Budget. Standard rate of income tax reduced from 33% to 30%, top rate from 83% to 60%. New unified VAT rate of 15% introduced.
1–8 August	Lusaka Commonwealth Conference: need for new Rhodesian constitution agreed. Constitution to be drawn up at conference at Lancaster House, London.
27 August	Mountbatten assassinated by IRA. Warrenpoint IRA bomb kills 18 soldiers.
29–30 November	Dublin EC Council: arguments about excessive British contribution to EC budget. Thatcher rejects offer of £350 million refund and Council ends in deadlock.
21 December	Lancaster House Conference ends with agreement over new Rhodesian constitution. Cease-fire declared: Soames takes over as Governor until elections in 1980.

1980

2 January	Steel strike begins.
12 March	Southend East by-election: Conservatives hold seat but majority reduced from 10,774 to 430.
26 March	Budget. Howe introduces MTFS as government's economic strategy
3 April	Steel strike ends as BSC management and unions agree to independent enquiry into pay.
27–28 April	Luxembourg EC Council: Thatcher offered refund of £760 million to solve budget crisis but rejects deal.
1 May	Privatisation of British Aerospace.

29 May	Carrington (Foreign Secretary) and Gilmour (Lord Privy Seal) secure deal reducing British contribution to EC budget: accepted by Cabinet on 2 June.
1 August	1980 Employment Bill enacted: secondary picketing outlawed and closed shop restricted.
8 August	1980 Housing Bill enacted: 'right to buy' for council house tenants introduced.
10 October	Thatcher's speech to Conservative party conference, Brighton. She will not abandon economic strategy: 'The lady's not for turning'.
10 November	Foot elected Labour Party leader.

1981

5 January	Cabinet reshuffle. St John Stevas and Maude dismissed. Pym moved from Defence to Leader of House of Commons. Nott takes over at Defence and Brittan enters Cabinet as Chief Secretary to the Treasury.
18 February	Government forced to withdraw plans for 23 coal pit closures in face of NUM strike threats.
10 March	Budget. Faced with deep recession Howe cuts public spending by £3,290 million and increases tax burden, although income tax rates are unchanged. Clearest break yet with Keynesian orthodoxy.
26 March	SDP formally launched by former Labour politicians: arranges electoral alliance with Liberal Party in September.
30 March	Petition from 364 leading academic economists calling for a return to Keynesian policies published by *The Times*.
11–14 April	Riots in Brixton.
5 May	Sands dies after 66 days of hunger strike: riots in Northern Ireland.
14 September	Cabinet reshuffle: purge of the 'wets'. Carlisle, Gilmour and Soames sacked; Prior reluctantly becomes Northern Ireland Secretary. Lawson, Tebbit and Parkinson, all committed Thatcherites, enter Cabinet.
3 October	IRA hunger strike ends: 10 strikers died during protest.
22 October	Croydon North West by-election: Alliance takes seat from Conservatives, winning majority of 3,254 (1979 Conservative majority was 3,769).
26 November	Crosby by-election: Alliance takes seat from Conservatives, winning majority of 5,289 (1979 Conservative majority was 19,272).

1982

2 April	Argentina invades Falkland Islands. British Cabinet approves dispatch of naval task force.

5 April	Carrington and two junior Foreign Office ministers resign over Falklands invasion and Thatcher appoints Pym as Foreign Secretary. Task force sails.
25 April	British forces recapture South Georgia. Thatcher tells reporters to 'Rejoice!'.
2 May	HMS *Conqueror* sinks *General Belgrano*: 321 lives lost.
14 June	British forces capture Port Stanley: Argentina surrenders.
28 October	1982 Employment Bill enacted: compensation provided for workers sacked after refusing to join a closed shop.

1983

9 June	Thatcher wins general election. Conservative majority: 144.
11 June	New government announced. Pym dismissed. Howe becomes Foreign Secretary and Lawson replaces him as Chancellor. Brittan becomes Home Secretary.
17–19 June	Stuttgart EC Council: Britain's excessive budget contribution returns to the agenda. Thatcher insists a long-term solution must be found.
2 October	Kinnock replaces Foot as Labour Party leader.
14 October	Parkinson resigns when row over affair with former secretary, Keays, refuses to abate. Tebbit replaces him at DTI.
24 October	US troops invade Grenada in response to Marxist coup. Thatcher not consulted.

1984

25 January	Howe announces complete ban on trade union membership at GCHQ.
6 March	MacGregor, NCB Chairman, confirms plans to close around 20 'uneconomic' coal pits.
12 March	NUM begins strike in protest at pit closures.
14–17 June	Fontainebleau EC Council: permanent settlement for Britain's budget contributions finally accepted by Thatcher. Budget crisis resolved.
16 June	Portsmouth by-election: Alliance takes seat from Conservatives, winning majority of 1,341 (1983 Conservative majority was 12,335.)
26 July	Trade Union Bill enacted: Trade Union immunities further restricted; secret ballots for union officers made compulsory.
12 October	IRA bomb explodes in Grand Hotel, Brighton. Fails to assassinate Thatcher, but Tebbit and Wakeham badly injured. Six people killed.
25 October	NUM assets sequestrated by High Court after NUM refused to pay £200,000 fine for contempt of court.

20 November	British Telecom becomes first public utility to be privatised. Share issue over-subscribed.

1985

5 March	NUM Executive votes to end miners' strike. Victory for government.
4 July	Brecon and Radnor by-election: Alliance take seat from Conservatives, winning majority of 559 (1983 Conservative majority was 8,784).
16 July	Local Government Bill enacted: GLC and metropolitan authorities abolished.
2 September	Cabinet reshuffle: Thatcher looks to improve presentation. Brittan demoted to DTI. Replaced at Home Office by Hurd. Tebbit becomes Party Chairman. Rees, Jenkin and Gowrie leave Cabinet. Clarke, MacGregor and Baker enter Cabinet.
16–23 October	Nassau CHOGM: Thatcher resists Commonwealth demands for wide-reaching sanctions on South Africa in protest at apartheid.
15 November	Thatcher signs Anglo-Irish Agreement at Hillsborough: gives Irish government a consultative role in governing Northern Ireland to outrage of Unionists. Gow resigns in protest.

1986

9 January	Westland: Heseltine resigns as Defence Secretary claiming Thatcher ignored collective Cabinet responsibility. Replaced by Younger.
24 January	Westland: Brittan resigns from DTI after admitting responsibility for leaked letter of 6 January. Replaced by Channon.
17 February	Britain and other EC countries sign Single European Act: aims to strengthen EC social and economic cohesion.
14 April	Shops Bill to legalise Sunday trading defeated in Commons despite three-line whip.
15 April	US raid on Libya using British-based aircraft: hostile international reaction.
8 May	Ryedale by-election: Alliance takes seat from Conservatives, winning 4,940 majority (1983 Conservative majority was 16,142).
3 August	Special London Commonwealth Summit on South Africa: Thatcher makes minimal concessions on sanctions and is widely condemned for intransigence.
8 December	British Gas privatised.

1987

11 June   Thatcher wins general election: Conservative majority: 101.

13 June   New government formed: Hailsham, Biffen, Jopling and Tebbit leave Cabinet. Parkinson, Wakeham, Major and Havers enter Cabinet. The three great offices of state remain unchanged.

19 October   Black Monday: £50 billion wiped off share values.

1988

10 January   Thatcher loses invaluable ally as Whitelaw resigns from Cabinet after a stroke.

3 March   SDP and Liberal parties formally merge, forming Social and Liberal Democrats. Ashdown elected leader by postal ballot.

15 March   Budget: Lawson cuts standard income tax rate from 27% to 25% and top rate from 60% to 40%. Delights Conservative MPs.

26 May   Employment Act enacted: dismissal for non-membership of a trade union classed as unfair dismissal in all circumstances; bans trade unions from disciplining members for refusing to strike, even if strike was backed by ballot; looks to improve internal union accountability.

29 July   Education Reform Act enacted: radical shake-up of education system, including introduction of National Curriculum and right for schools to opt out of local authority control and manage their own budgets.

20 September   Bruges speech: Thatcher spells out strong anti-federalist stance for Britain in relation to EC.

1989

1 April   Community Charge introduced in Scotland: very unpopular and significant non-payment problem.

15 June   European Parliament elections: sweeping losses for Conservatives as Labour gains majority of UK European seats for first time ever.

24 July   Cabinet reshuffle: Howe removed from Foreign Office to become Leader of House of Commons and Deputy Prime Minister. Major becomes Foreign Secretary; Baker becomes Party Chairman. Moore, Channon, Young and Younger leave Cabinet.

26 October   Lawson resigns as Chancellor: claims that public opposition to his policies from Walters, Thatcher's personal economic advisor, has made his position impossible. Major becomes Chancellor; Hurd moves to Foreign Office.

5 December	Thatcher defeats Meyer's 'stalking horse' challenge for Conservative Party leadership by 314 votes to Meyer's 33. Abstentions: 27.

1990

1 April	Community Charge begins in England and Wales.
14 July	Ridley resigns after ill-judged remarks on Germany and EC in *Spectator* interview. Replaced at DTI by Lilley.
30 July	Gow murdered by IRA car bomb.
2 August	Iraq invades Kuwait: Thatcher gives press conference with Bush in Aspen, Colorado, calling for Iraqi withdrawal.
3 October	German reunification.
8 October	Sterling joins ERM at rate of DM2.95. UK interest rates cut by 1% to 14% at Thatcher's insistence.
18 October	Eastbourne by-election: Liberal Democrats take seat from Conservatives, winning majority of 4,550 (1987 Conservative majority was 16,923).
1 November	Howe resigns from government over Thatcher's handling of European policy.
	Employment Act enacted: makes refusing employment on grounds of trade union membership or non-membership unlawful; ends union immunities from civil damages claims for all forms of secondary action.
13 November	Howe's resignation speech: scathing attack on Thatcher's leadership. Her position badly damaged.
14 November	Heseltine announces intention to challenge Thatcher for leadership.
20 November	Conservative Party leadership election first ballot: Thatcher gains 204 votes to Heseltine's 152; 16 abstentions. Thatcher four votes short of margin required for outright victory: declares she will fight on in second ballot.
22 November	Thatcher announces she will not contest second ballot: Major and Hurd enter race.
28 November	Thatcher resigns: Major becomes new PM.

GLOSSARY

Assisted Places Scheme The scheme introduced in 1980 providing government funds to enable selected talented children, whose parents could not otherwise afford the fees, to attend private schools.

Central Policy Review Staff (CPRS) The government's internal think tank set up by Edward Heath in 1970. The CPRS was abolished by Mrs Thatcher in 1983 as the PM's Policy Unit assumed the dominant role on formulating policy ideas.

Centre for Policy Studies (CPS) The right-wing free market think tank founded in 1974 by Margaret Thatcher and Keith Joseph. Although formally independent of government, the CPS played a key role in guiding government policy in the early 1980s.

Closed shop A place of work in which all employees are required to belong to one particular trade union.

Collective Cabinet responsibility The doctrine that requires free discussion of issues in Cabinet, but that such discussions are kept secret. Furthermore, once the Cabinet agrees a stance on a particular issue, ministers must publicly support this stance.

Common Agricultural Policy (CAP) The agreement within the EC that maintains high prices for agricultural commodities, thus preserving employment for European farmers, many of whom would go out of business if prices were allowed to fall to a competitive level.

European Monetary Union (EMU) The unification of European currencies, which are replaced by a single European currency. Each country yields its independence to decide monetary policy to a European Central Bank, which determines monetary policy for the whole of the European Union.

European Currency Unit (ECU) A unit of currency that consisted of a bundle of different fixed proportions of the different currencies of EMS member countries. Never issued in paper form, the ECU was used for certain transactions between EC governments.

European Monetary System (EMS)   The system of economic co-operation adopted in 1979 by the then EC member countries, providing for the introduction of the ECU and the ERM.

Exchange Rate Mechanism (ERM)   The system whereby European governments attempted to achieve exchange rate stability by declaring approximate parities for their currencies which they were committed to defending.

General Agreement on Tariffs and Trade (GATT)   The international agreement of 1948, whereby many countries agreed to successively reduce tariffs and trade restrictions. Since 1948 there has been a series of GATT rounds, at which countries have gradually furthered free trade.

GP fundholding   The arrangement giving GPs their own budget, which they have to use to 'buy' treatment for their patients from the relevant service providers. Hospitals are thus in competition with each other to provide efficient, value-for-money services that will attract GPs' 'business'.

Grant maintained school   A school that chooses to 'opt out' of local authority control and receive funding directly from central government. Control over how to spend the school's budget passes from the local authority to the school's governing body.

Incomes policy   The direct attempt by government, through legislation or implicit pressure, to influence the level of wages and other incomes. Although popular with many governments since the war, incomes policy was rejected by the Thatcher government and has not been used since.

International Monetary Fund (IMF)   Established in 1944 as an agency of the United Nations, the IMF aims to promote co-operation and free trade among its members. Through members' subscriptions, it has accumulated currency reserves, which are available to member countries with balance of payments crises. Under the Callaghan government (1976–79), Britain was forced to apply for such a loan.

Keynesianism   The economic theory dating back to John Maynard Keynes. Keynesians believed that government economic policy should focus on fiscal measures, 'fine tuning' demand in the economy to mitigate adverse cyclical effects such as high levels of unemployment.

Monetarism   In the 1950s and 1960s, as inflation and unemployment rose at the same time, monetarism developed as an alternative to Keynesianism. Led by Milton Freedman, monetarists denied that governments could influence long-term unemployment through tinkering with demand. Government intervention in the economy should be minimised and limited to controlling the money supply, which monetarists claimed would ensure a low inflation rate, and to supply-side measures to maximise economic efficiency.

Organisation for Economic Co-operation and Development (OECD) Established in 1961 by 20 economically developed countries, the OECD aims to co-ordinate the economic policy of its members and promote economic growth, employment and prosperity within member countries.

Pluralism Pluralism requires that a society has a number of different political groups, among whom power and influence are shared with no group alone being able to determine all decisions affecting life within the society.

Public Sector Borrowing Requirement (PSBR) The total budget deficit of central and local government combined with any losses made by nationalised industries.

Secondary picketing Gatherings of strikers at premises where employees are not yet on strike to demonstrate and persuade these employees to join the strike. Particularly in the coal industry, there were many instances of violent secondary pickets physically preventing others from working.

Strategic Defence Initiative (SDI) Proposed by Ronald Reagan in 1983, SDI aimed to provide the USA with total protection against nuclear attack by intercepting incoming ballistic missiles long before they reached their target. Although seen as accelerating the arms race, it later emerged that SDI (dubbed 'Star Wars') was more science fiction than a realistic proposition.

Wets Thatcher's opponents within the Conservative Party who did not share her faith in monetarism. 'Wet' was intended to suggest that her opponents were too feeble to endure the short-term unpopularity of harsh public spending cuts which Thatcher saw as essential for long-term economic prosperity.

GUIDE TO CHARACTERS

Ashdown, Paddy   British Liberal politician; founding leader of the Liberal Democrats (1988–99), after the SDP and Liberal parties merged.

Baker, Kenneth   British Conservative politician; Education Secretary (1986–89); Party Chairman (1989–90).

Brittan, Leon   British Conservative politician; Chief Secretary to the Treasury (1981–83); Home Secretary (1983–85); Trade and Industry Secretary (1985–86). Resigned over the Westland Affair. European Commissioner (1989–99).

Brooke, Peter   British Conservative politician; Party Chairman (1987–89); Northern Ireland Secretary (1989–92).

Bush, George   US Republican politician; US President (1989–93).

Callaghan, James   British Labour politician; Prime Minister (1976–79); party leader (1976–80).

Carrington, Peter   British Conservative politician; Foreign Secretary (1979–82). Resigned over Argentina's invasion of the Falkland Islands.

Foot, Michael   British Labour politician; party leader (1980–83).

Gilmour, Ian   British Conservative politician; Lord Privy Seal (1979–81). Sacked in the second purge of the 'wets' (September 1981).

Giscard d'Estaing, Valery   French centrist politician; French President (1974–81).

Gorbachev, Mikhail   Soviet politician; Soviet President (1985–91).

Gow, Ian   British Conservative politician; PPS to Prime Minister (1979–83) and enjoyed close personal relationship with Mrs Thatcher. Murdered by IRA in 1990.

Gummer, John   British Conservative politician; Party Chairman (1983–85); agriculture minister (1989–92).

Heath, Edward   British Conservative politician; Prime Minister (1970–74); party leader (1965–75). Lost 1975 leadership election to Mrs Thatcher.

Heseltine, Michael   British Conservative politician; Environment Secretary (1979–83); Defence Secretary (1983–86). Walked out of Cabinet over Westland Affair, 1986; challenged Mrs Thatcher for party leadership leading to John Major becoming Prime Minister in 1990.

Howe, Geoffrey   British Conservative politician; Chancellor of the Exchequer (1979–83); Foreign Secretary (1983–89); Leader of the House of Commons and Deputy Prime Minister (1989–90). Resigned in protest at Mrs Thatcher's style of government and Eurosceptical policy stance.

Hurd, Douglas   British Conservative politician; Northern Ireland Secretary (1984–85); Home Secretary (1985–89); Foreign Secretary (1989–95).

Ingham, Bernard   British civil servant; Chief Press Secretary (1979–90).

Jenkins, Roy   British Liberal politician; founding leader of SDP (1982–83).

Joseph, Keith   British Conservative politician; Industry Secretary (1979–81); Education Secretary (1981–86). Intellectual heavyweight who played a key role in defining what Thatcherism stood for.

Kinnock, Neil   British Labour politician; party leader (1983–92).

Kohl, Helmut   German Christian Democrat politician; German Chancellor (1982–98).

Lawson, Nigel   British Conservative politician; Energy Secretary (1981–83); Chancellor of the Exchequer (1983–89). Resigned after Mrs Thatcher refused to sack her economic advisor Alan Walters.

Major, John   British Conservative politician; Chief Secretary to the Treasury (1987–89); Foreign Secretary (1989); Chancellor of the Exchequer (1989–90); party leader and Prime Minister (1990–98).

Mitterrand, François   French Socialist politician; French President (1981–95).

Moore, John   British Conservative politician; Transport Secretary (1986–87); Health and Social Security Secretary (1987–88); Social Security Secretary (1988–89). Once seen as possible successor to Mrs Thatcher but his health crumbled in 1988.

Neave, Airey   British Conservative politician; managed Mrs Thatcher's campaign for the party leadership (1975). Murdered by INLA in 1979.

Parkinson, Cecil   British Conservative politician; Party Chairman (1981–83); Trade and Industry Secretary (1983). Resigned over affair with his secretary. Energy Secretary (1987–89); Transport Secretary (1989–90).

Powell, Charles   British civil servant; Private Secretary to the Prime Minister (1984–91). One of Mrs Thatcher's most trusted advisors.

Prior, James   British Conservative politician; Employment Secretary (1979–81); Northern Ireland Secretary (1981–84).

Pym, Francis   British Conservative politician; Defence Secretary (1979–81); Leader of the House of Commons (1981–82); Foreign Secretary (1982–83).

Reagan, Ronald   US Republican politician; US President (1981–89).

Ridley, Nicholas   British Conservative politician; Transport Secretary (1983–85); Environment Secretary (1986–89); Trade and Industry Secretary (1989–90). Resigned after making ill-judged comments about Germany.

Schmidt, Helmut   German Socialist politician; German Chancellor (1979–82).

Soames, Christopher   British Conservative politician; last Governor of Rhodesia (1979–80); Leader of the House of Lords (1979–81). Sacked in the second purge of the 'wets' (September 1981).

Stevas, Norman St John   British Conservative politician; Leader of the House of Commons (1979–81). First 'wet' to be dismissed by Mrs Thatcher.

Tebbit, Norman   British Conservative politician; Employment Secretary (1981–83); Trade and Industry Secretary (1983–85); Party Chairman (1985–87).

Thatcher, Margaret   British Conservative politician; Education Secretary (1970–74); leader of Conservative Party (1975–90); Prime Minister (1979–90).

Thorneycroft, Peter   British Conservative politician; Party Chairman (1979–81).

Waddington, David   British Conservative politician; Chief Whip (1987–89); Home Secretary (1989–90).

Wakeham, John   British Conservative politician; Chief Whip (1982–87); Leader of the House of Commons (1987–89); Energy Secretary (1989–90). Managed Mrs Thatcher's leadership election campaign in 1990.

Walker, Peter   British Conservative politician; Agriculture Secretary (1979–83); Energy Secretary (1983–87); Welsh Secretary (1987–90).

Walters, Alan   British economist; personal economic advisor to the Prime Minister (1981–84, 1989). Resigned after Lawson quit as Chancellor in protest at Walters' open criticism of government policy.

Whitelaw, William   British Conservative politician; Home Secretary (1979–83); Leader of the House of Lords (1983–88); *de facto* Deputy Prime Minister (1979–88).

BIBLIOGRAPHY

PRIMARY SOURCES

A wealth of primary source material for the Thatcher era can be found in contemporary press articles. Not only does the press provide an indication of contemporary reaction to the government's performance, but many papers also regularly feature analysis by political commentators. This analysis provides instant political history, which is of great value to the modern historian.

The papers that are of most use are the following:

1 *The Daily Telegraph.*
2 *The Guardian.*
3 *The Independent.*
4 *The Times.*
5 *The Financial Times.*
6 *The Observer.*
7 *The Sunday Telegraph.*
8 *The Sunday Times.*

Weekly political journals are also of interest. The most useful articles for an introduction to the Thatcher years are contained in the following three:

9 *The Economist.*
10 *The New Statesman.*
11 *The Spectator.*

There has been a blossoming of ministerial memoirs from those at the heart of the Thatcher administrations. Together with the memoirs of others, these form an invaluable primary source, although some are far more candid and thus more useful to the historian than others. (Note: the place of publication is London unless otherwise stated.)

12 Baker, K., *The Turbulent Years*, Faber and Faber, 1993.

13   Clark, A., *Diaries*, Phoenix, 1994.
14   Cole, J., *As It Seemed To Me*, Phoenix, 1996.
15   Fowler, N., *Ministers Decide*, Chapmans, 1991.
16   Gilmour, I., *Dancing with Dogma*, Simon and Schuster, 1992.
17   Hattersley, R., *Who Goes Home?*, Warner, 1996.
18   Hayek, F., *The Road to Serfdom*, Routledge, 1944.
19   Healey, D., *The Time of My Life*, Penguin, 1990.
20   Heath, E., *The Course of My Life*, Hodder and Stoughton, 1998.
21   Howe, G., *Conflict of Loyalty*, Macmillan, 1994.
22   Ingham, B., *Kill the Messenger*, Fontana, 1991.
23   Lawson, N., *The View from No. 11*, Bantam Press, 1992.
24   Parkinson, C., *Right at the Centre*, Weidenfeld and Nicolson, 1992.
25   Prior, J., *A Balance of Power*, Hamish Hamilton, 1986.
26   Ridley, N., *My Style of Government*, Hutchinson, 1991.
27   Tebbit, N., *Upwardly Mobile*, Weidenfeld and Nicolson, 1988.
28   Thatcher, M., *The Downing Street Years*, HarperCollins, 1993.
29   Thatcher, M., *The Path to Power*, HarperCollins, 1995.
30   Thatcher, M., *The Collected Speeches*, HarperCollins, 1997.
31   Walker, P., *Staying Power*, Bloomsbury, 1991.
32   Whitelaw, W., *The Whitelaw Memoirs*, Aurum Press, 1989.
33   Woodward, S., *One Hundred Days*, HarperCollins, 1992.

SECONDARY SOURCES

34   Adonis, A. and Hames, T. (eds), *A Conservative Revolution: The Thatcher–Reagan Decade*, Manchester University Press, Manchester, 1994.
35   Ball, S. and Seldon, A. (eds), *Conservative Century: The Conservative Party since 1900*, Oxford University Press, Oxford, 1994.
36   Ball, S. and Seldon, A. (eds), *The Heath Government 1970–74*, Addison Wesley Longman, Harlow, 1996.
37   Butler, D. and Butler, G., *British Political Facts 1900–1994*, Macmillan, 1994.
38   Butler, D. and Kavanagh, D., *The British General Election of 1979*, Macmillan, 1980.
39   Butler, D. and Kavanagh, D., *The British General Election of 1983*, Macmillan, 1984.
40   Butler, D. and Kavanagh, D., *The British General Election of 1987*, Macmillan, 1988.
41   Butler, D., Adonis, A. and Travers, T., *Failure in British Government*, Oxford University Press, Oxford, 1994.
42   Crick, M., *Michael Heseltine: A Biography*, Penguin, 1997.
43   Evans, E., *Thatcher and Thatcherism*, Routledge, 1997.
44   Gamble, A., *The Free Economy and the Strong State*, Macmillan, 1994.
45   Hall, J. and Jacques, M. (eds), *The Politics of Thatcherism*, Lawrence and Wishart, 1983.

46   Harris, K., *Thatcher*, Weidenfeld and Nicolson, 1988.
47   Hattersley, R., *Fifty Years On*, Little, Brown and Co., 1997.
48   Hennessy, P., *The Hidden Wiring*, Victor Gollancz, 1995.
49   Hennessy, P. and Seldon, A. (eds), *Ruling Performance*, Basil
     Blackwell, Oxford, 1987.
50   Holmes, M., *The First Thatcher Government 1979–1983*, Wheatsheaf,
     Brighton, 1985.
51   Holmes, M., *Thatcherism: Scope and Limits 1983–87*, Macmillan,
     1989.
52   Jenkins, P., *Mrs Thatcher's Revolution*, Jonathan Cape, 1987.
53   Jenkins, S., 'Tear up the Tory Clause Four', *The Times*, 12.10.94,
     p. 18.
54   Jenkins, S., *Accountable to None: The Tory Nationalisation of Britain*,
     Penguin, 1996.
55   Johnson, C., *The Economy under Mrs Thatcher*, Penguin, 1991.
56   Kavanagh, D., *Thatcherism and British Politics*, Oxford University
     Press, Oxford, 1987.
57   Kavanagh, D., 'The Legacy of Thatcherism', *Contemporary Record*,
     Vol. 3, No. 1 (Autumn 1989), pp. 16–17.
58   Kavanagh, D. and Seldon A. (eds), *The Thatcher Effect*, Oxford
     University Press, Oxford, 1989.
59   Kavanagh, D. and Seldon, A. (eds), *The Major Effect*, Macmillan,
     1994.
60   Keegan, W., *Mrs Thatcher's Economic Experiment*, Allen Lane, 1984.
61   Letwin, S. R., *The Anatomy of Thatcherism*, Fontana, 1992.
62   Marquand, D. and Seldon, A. (eds), *The Ideas that Shaped Postwar
     Britain*, Fontana, 1996.
63   Minogue, K. and Biddis, M., *Thatcherism: Personality and Politics*,
     Macmillan, 1987.
64   Morgan, K., *The People's Peace*, Oxford University Press, Oxford,
     1990.
65   Pimlott, B., 'The Unimportance of Thatcherism', *Contemporary
     Record*, Vol. 3, No. 1 (Autumn 1989), pp. 89–110.
66   Riddell, P., *The Thatcher Government*, Basil Blackwell, Oxford, 1983.
67   Riddell, P., *The Thatcher Era*, Basil Blackwell, Oxford, 1991.
68   Seldon, A., 'An Interview with Keith Joseph', *Contemporary Record*,
     Vol. 1, No.1 (Spring 1987), pp. 26–31.
69   Seldon, A. (ed.), *How Tory Governments Fall*, Fontana, 1996.
70   Seldon, A., *Major: A Political Life*, Weidenfeld and Nicolson, 1997.
71   Seldon, A., *Ten Downing Street*, HarperCollins, 1999.
72   Siedentop, L., 'Thatcherism and the Constitution', *The Times Literary
     Supplement*, 26.1.90, pp. 88 and 99.
73   Skidelsky, R. (ed.), *Thatcherism*, Chatto and Windus, 1988.
74   Thatcher, C., *Below the Parapet*, HarperCollins, 1997.
75   Walters, A., *Britain's Economic Renaissance*, Oxford University Press,
     Oxford, 1986.

76   Young, H., *One of Us*, Pan Books, 1993.
77   Young, H. and Sloman, A., *The Thatcher Phenomenom*, BBC Books, 1986.

Although published too late for use in research for this book, 1999 sees the publication by Oxford University Press of Margaret Thatcher's complete statements 1945–90, (7,500 in all) in CD-ROM format (ed. Christopher Collins). This should prove an invaluable resource for future students of Margaret Thatcher and her governments.

INDEX